PRAISE FOR ~~STRESSED~~ LEADERS

I found ~~Stressed~~ Leaders: Stay in the Game to be incredibly valuable and practical. Dan Stecken shares personal stories and hard-won wisdom, offering tangible strategies for managing stress, setting boundaries, and prioritizing well-being. It's more than just identifying problems; it provides solutions. The book's emphasis on self-care, building resilience, and finding support systems is crucial for any leader. This is a must-read for anyone navigating the complexities of leadership and seeking to thrive both professionally and personally.

Michael Lubelfeld
Superintendent, Author, Consultant

Too many leadership books live in theory – this one lives in truth. Dan invites us into the real, raw experience of leading when it's hard, lonely, and heavy. It's not polished or performative – it's honest. And that's what makes it powerful. This isn't just a book for leaders who want to grow; it's for those who want to stay human while doing it. Dan gives us permission to be unfinished, while still being impactful. It's a guide, a mirror, and a reminder of why we chose this work in the first place.

PJ Caposey
Superintendent, Author, Keynote, Coach

For school leaders silently carrying the weight of it all – this book sees you, and it helps you come home to yourself.

Danny Bauer
Chief Ruckus Maker, Bestselling Author
International Speaker

Simply put, we have leaders who are going in every day and dying on the vine. They're burned out and lack the support necessary to reset and decrease the allostatic load that's developed. Dan doesn't just give the same jargon that we always see; this book finally provides leaders with tangible and actionable ways that they can take OWNERSHIP of their mental wellbeing. I know I am better for having read this, and I believe you will be too.

Dr. Joe Mullikin
Educator, Speaker, Leadership Consultant

Dan doesn't just write about leadership – he lives it. ~~Stressed Leaders~~ is raw, honest, and exactly what burned-out leaders need right now. I've worked alongside Dan and seen firsthand the passion and conviction behind his words. This book is a lifeline for anyone who feels the weight of leadership pressing down. It's vulnerable, practical, and deeply motivating. If you lead others and feel like you're drowning in the mess, this book will help you rise again – with clarity, courage, and purpose.

Petie Kinder
Pastor

Leadership doesn't have to cost you everything. Dan gets it because he's lived it. He's done it all, teacher, head coach, administrator, superintendent, husband, father. He's been in the fire, not watching from a distance. This book doesn't just give you a motivational pat on the back – it gives you real, tangible tools to fill your cup, take back your energy, mindset, and your purpose.

If you're tired of wearing "busy" like a badge, then you're ready to take a breath and open Dan's book, ~~Stressed~~ Leaders. It's the book we've all been waiting for – one that understands the daily pressure we face as leaders, trying to do it all. Because the truth is: leadership does not come from running on empty – it comes from leading with a full tank.

Jonathan Alsheimer
Teacher, Speaker, Author

I am extremely proud of Dan Stecken for the powerful work he has done in this remarkable book, *~~Stressed~~ Leaders Stay in the Game*. As a former Physical Education & Health teacher who later became a principal, I understand firsthand the physical and emotional demands that leadership places on an individual. Dan not only acknowledges these challenges – he equips leaders with the tools to navigate them with resilience and purpose.

Dan shares personal experiences and insights that are as compelling as they are instructive. If you're a current or aspiring school or district leader seeking longevity, vitality, and emotional and physical stamina, this book is for you. Dan's message is timely, transformational, and needed in the field of education.

Dr. Don Parker
Former Principal, Educational Consultant, Author

In *~~Stressed~~ Leaders*, Dan Stecken reminds us that while leadership comes with stress, it also reveals the greatness within us. Through honest storytelling, practical tools, and grounded wisdom, Dan encourages leaders to stay true to their purpose. He shows that challenges are not roadblocks but fuel for growth. This book is an inspiring guide for anyone looking to lead with impact and resilience.

Brandon Beck
Speaker, Teacher, Leadership Coach

This is not another self help book filled with "ideals" that sound great in theory but hold no weight in practice. Dan expertly strings together the lessons he's learned from decades of leadership as a superintendent and practical actions to leave the reader feeling not just inspired but empowered to implement these changes into their own life. You can tell that Dan channeled his years of coaching sports into his writing, because the whole book leaves you feeling like you're back at practice, learning lessons from a coach who cares more about your development as a person, then just an athlete – the BEST type of coach. Anyone who holds a position of leadership NEEDS to dive into this book.

Michael Donatelli
Personal Trainer/Nutrition Coach

~~Stressed~~ *Leaders: Stay in the Game,* by Dan Stecken, is a must read for any school leader feeling overwhelmed by the relentless demands of the job. With honesty, heart, and practical strategies, Dan offers a lifeline to those on the edge, reminding us that burnout isn't the end – it's a signal for change.

Glenn Robbins
Award-Winning Educational Leader, Best-Selling Author, Speaker

Raw, real, honest and reflective, Dan Stecken delivers hard truth and real strategies in ~~Stressed~~ *Leaders: Stay in the Game*. It's honest, unfiltered, and exactly what school leaders need. This book is the perfect combination of a gut check and a guide – most of all, it's inspiring. If you've ever felt overwhelmed in leadership, Dan reminds you that you're not alone and you can rise through the mess. This is a must read for anyone in leadership.

Courtney Orzel
Superintendent, Author, Speaker

Every school leader has that moment when they wonder if the stress and anxiety are worth it. ~~Stressed~~ *Leaders* reminds us why the work matters and how to keep going when it gets tough. School leadership is an incredible calling, and the more people we can keep in it, the better our schools will be. Dan offers not just inspiration to start strong but practical, doable habits to stay in the game. His approach is grounded, relatable, and exactly what leaders need to keep moving forward.

Joe Sanfelippo
Retired Superintendent, Author, Speaker

~~stressed~~ LEADERS
Stay in the Game

Dan Stecken

~~stressed~~ Leaders: Stay in the Game

Copyright © by Dan Stecken
First Edition 2025

All rights reserved.

No part of this publication may be reproduced in any form, or by any means, electronic or mechanical, including photocopying, recording, or any information browsing, storage or retrieval system, without permission in writing from the publisher.

Road to Awesome, LLC.

DEDICATION

I would like to formally dedicate this work to my children, Camryn and Costner. In 2008, my life changed forever, then in 2012, it completely changed again as I held each one of my children in my arms at their birth. They are my greatest accomplishments. They have given me some of the best memories and cherished moments of my life. I have lived my Stressed Leaders journey along with them and for them, trying to be the greatest role model I can be. The job of Dad is my favorite and one that I am most proud of.

I would also like to thank some critical leaders who gave great advice and help in this journey. My strength training and fitness coach, Mike Donatelli, has one of the best vibes of any other guy I've ever met. He has been a constant motivating force for me along my weight loss journey and my progress in achieving goals, stacking bricks, and building myself into the man I am proud of today. As an older guy traversing the Do Hard Things world, I loved developing this journey along with his advice and wisdom. The world is a better place with men like Mike leading, supporting, and empowering others.

Finally, to my rock, my wife, Karie. She's been my biggest supporter and best fan. Riding side by side through all of the crazy journeys she has been pulled along, she's been there, supporting and being the better half of our couple. From starting a travel softball and baseball program as an under appreciated head coach's wife, to being a key leader in our ~~Stressed~~ Leaders journey, Karie has been there to support my dreams from day one. Her warm welcoming personality makes everyone love her, and she is the truest servant leader I know. She will do anything to help anyone, above her own needs. I couldn't love this woman any more, even on the days I don't show it enough because of the mess. She is what keeps our mess clean and our lives so warm and sunny each day.

TABLE OF CONTENTS

Introduction — 1

Chapter 1 — 13
~~Stressed~~ Leaders Shock the System

Chapter 2 — 25
~~Stressed~~ Leaders Go First

Chapter 3 — 53
~~Stressed~~ Leaders Serve Others

Chapter 4 — 67
~~Stressed~~ Leaders Do Hard Things

Chapter 5 — 81
~~Stressed~~ Leaders Need Community

Conclusion — 91
~~Stressed~~ Leaders Need Perspective

Afterword — 99
~~Stressed~~ Leaders Retreat

About the Author — 107

INTRODUCTION

> "If you continue to push this referendum to close our school, we will hurt you and your family."
>
> Signed-
> "A taxpayer in OUR district"

Twenty years of being an educational leader did not prepare me for the tone of the conversation I was about to have that day with another district leader. As colleagues and friends, we discussed a number of items on our call, typical small talk: how are your kids, how's your school year going, etc. But when this man told me he had received multiple death threats in his mailbox at his house, I had to catch my breath. This leader is one of the smartest men I have come across in my leadership journey. A well-read, articulate leader of his district, I had come to know this man as a passionate leader of his community and a pillar in our Superintendent community. His voice ratcheted up with anger as he described personal attacks and direct threats to his home and family. Can you imagine explaining this to your spouse and children? Their home is no longer a safe space, panic and anxiety building up in your family, and your responsibilities to control that situation are now of the utmost importance. Before I could even get to the deeper questions, he told me, "I'm fu**ing done."

We are passionate leaders, doing our best to lead our districts, students, staff, and community members. We make tough decisions, have difficult conversations, and make strategic plans, amongst other duties, but to have someone threaten your life, your family, and your livelihood over a decision you made is difficult to stomach. It eats at you. It consumes your mind. Everyone handles it differently, some cry, some bury it deep inside of them, some react with anger, while others wallow in their misery.

I don't care what kind of a leader you are or what wars you've been through. When someone threatens your life, your family's well being, or your home, it's a gut punch. As my friend opened up to me about what he was going through, I felt enraged. My claws were coming out, ready to ravage. I wanted to fight for him, to help him scratch his way through this troubling time. As his anger retreated to a more somber tone, almost melancholy, he somewhat nonchalantly said, "Well that's what we do. We deal with all the bullshit."

Why do we allow ourselves to be the punching bag so often in our leadership journeys? I refused to allow him to shut down, to close himself off, and reminded him that if he needed anything, I was ready and willing to be there for him. As we ended the call, I already knew he wasn't going to reach out about it again. He didn't want me to think he was weak, which couldn't have been further from the reality of what I was currently thinking: *Here's a man struggling to manage his emotions right now, and he wants to make it seem like all is OK. All is not OK! Someone is threatening him and his family, sending garbage like that to his home.* But I knew before he hung up the phone that he had resigned himself to defeat, that it was OK to just accept these terms from an outsider – a cowardly, anonymous one at that. What happens when our leadership roles add layers of stress to our lives, that instead of bringing fulfillment, sends us to a dark place like my friend?

This book is real. It is raw. It is vulnerable. It is a testament to one man's journey of admitting his own failures as a leader, man, husband, father, and leader in a school district. It isn't meant to be rainbows and sunshine or meaningless leadership cheerleading, rather it is the truth. As Stressed Leaders, we put ourselves out there, with a big bullseye on our backs to, unfortunately, face the reality my friend was struggling to navigate. It isn't fair; it isn't gracious, but sadly, it can happen to any of us. Parents can sometimes lose rational thought when their children are impacted. Our faculty and staff will typically only see the world through their eyes, not understanding the minutia and variables of our decision-making, only how it impacts *them*.

Regardless of the decisions made and the outcomes, many people don't take the time to think about the decision-making process, facts, or events. Rather they are hijacked by the moment, by their emotions. Rarely do they consider the person making the decisions, the sweat equity that leader has built up with years of hard work and servant leadership. It is our reality as transformational leaders to manage the situation, the people, the events, and the outcomes – good and bad – and to continue working and thriving. We strive to support our teachers, our paraprofessionals, our support staff, to put them in the best situations for the betterment of our students. We spend countless hours attempting to build and scaffold support systems for our people who are taking care of our kids. But who is there to support the leaders? Who is there to make the time to support the leaders of our buildings and our school districts? How long can you stay confident – thriving in spite of setbacks, attacks, or failures?

I once went through a career-challenging dilemma. A confidential discipline matter needed solutions. As the Superintendent, I was a part of the investigation and needed to respect the privacy of everyone involved. Outsiders weren't entitled to all of the details due to personnel matters and privacy requirements, which is often the case when controversial decisions are made. So, they had filled in gaps with their own narratives. They wanted blood. The sharks were circling the chum bucket of my life, muddying the waters with my own blood. Twenty years of a career didn't matter; twenty years of dedication to a school district and community was not important to this group of parents. They wanted justice for a situation in which they didn't have all the facts. They wanted me gone.

In school leadership, we talk about taking care of the ones who take care of our students. It is critical as a school administrator to support, empower, and care for our teachers and support staff. In my fourth year as a Superintendent, I had to have a difficult conversation with a teacher, a long-tenured veteran. She chastised me for not checking in on her enough. I ate it; it hurt. I took it personally. She was not wrong, however. For years, board reports, project management, facility improvements, and organizational change were my focus, and I ended up distancing myself from relationships, the purpose of my career. It was a great opportunity for a reset, a reminder of why I do what I do.

But who is there to take care of the leaders when the leaders are suffering? Who is there to support the Stressed Leader who feels isolated and has nobody to turn to for support? Besides our loved ones at home, who is there to throw a life preserver to the Stressed Leader who is drowning? Who exists to throw a life saver to the leader who continues to isolate himself during trying times? From the nervous energy, the panic of being caught as a prisoner of the moment to the anger that can swell in tough times, these moments can be mentally, sometimes physically, crippling. Have you ever lived in this moment, nobody to turn to who truly understands that lonely chair you sit in, during a time of crisis? As leaders, we sit in that chair with the weight of the world on our shoulders, feeling like our chin is barely above the rising water that is threatening to drown us. Who checks in on the leaders? Average people resign themselves to a defeated fate, while elite leaders become emboldened to set their sights even higher, in the face of such setbacks.

Every superintendent, principal, or other school administrator tires of the comment, "That's why you make the big bucks." This logic is beyond frustrating. Because you make a decent living, typically still below corporate management level, does that mean you deserve to be defecated upon? You've earned the right to be everyone else's punching bag? Somehow, you've earned your place as the dumpster for others' vitriol? Parents want their districts to succeed and be great places for their children to grow, but the all-too-common validation and justification of the mistreatment of leaders needs to stop. Who is there to support those who fight the daily battles, the grind of angry parents, the apathetic kids, the unsatisfactory employee, or the community members out for blood? Sadly, there aren't many resources to help, not too many shoulders to lean on, not enough hugs to be given, and fewer voices to reach out to. There are all sorts of books meant to support leaders, anti-stress strategies are rampant on social media channels, and hopefully, you have some people in your local network you can call, email, or grab lunch with. But is that enough? What if there was a way to go from being a Stressed Leader to a ~~Stressed~~ Leader? What if there was a movement of people, an at-your-fingertips network to huddle up with or a physical in-person retreat to immerse yourself in real practical strategies of support?

For over twenty years, I have been writing emails, journaling, reflecting, and developing far too many ideas for books that are yet to be completed. Most of my problem statements or pain points that guide my writing and consume my thoughts center around leadership in crisis. During this span of time, I've also been an educator, a classroom teacher, a hall of fame varsity head coach, a chief school business official, and a school district superintendent. Throughout that span of time there was always a mess. And let me tell you, that mess can consume you, destroy your mind, and impact your family through your reactions. That mess will control your mood, it will consume your personality, and it will occupy 99% of your daily thoughts. Our mental strength has never been under so much attack as it is in today's age. The constant attacks on social media and the distractions that take us away from the successes we strive for continue to grow. But why? Why do we allow ourselves to let this happen to us? It's quite simple really: Because we care. We went into the business of leading others to support other people and bring out the best in them. When the worst comes out and is thrown on our desk or in our faces because of something we did, that mess will own any leader.

- a problem student struggling with a horrible home life situation
- a player who looks up to you like a father figure, whose home life is unraveling while going through their parents' messy divorce

- a tax problem that needed long-term strategic budgeting and forecasting analysis, but the numbers just did not add up – the solutions meant impacting someone's livelihood
- the parent group who wanted to come after your job, to see you burn – as the man in the hot seat with the bullseye on his back, that target intensifies as the pressure mounts

These four hypothetical events, unfortunately, are all too real for most leaders and our solutions to these problems can be messy. When we live in the mess it is incredibly easy to obsessively and compulsively drown in it. In his book *Lead From Where You Are*, accomplished author and retired Superintendent Joe Sanfelippo wrote, "When we live in the mess there has to be a way to tease out the amazing moments that happen in your space on a day-to-day basis." Those moments happen in a great school district all of the time. I've been blessed to lead a district, whose pride is unmatched, whose culture is unrivaled. It takes daily conscious effort to promote our school culture; it doesn't just happen magically. While it is authentic, it takes effort to continue to build upon it. But building any successful program, culture, or change takes time and takes intentional and consistent effort. Like trust, these movements take years to build but seconds to break when under attack.

But all the positivity in a culture is also always under attack. There is always that parent who feels like their kid didn't get a fair shake. There will always be that handful of disgruntled employees who refuse to buy in, no matter how great the growth is. They sit together, in the shadows and stir the cauldron of negativity, sucking life from the organization. Perhaps you have a board member who is more concerned with promoting their agenda that attempts to hijack your cultural growth.

How do we combat the attacks on our culture? How do we find the amazing moments, tease out the growth, and celebrate the success? It takes effort and intention to grow the culture and to recognize incremental growth. It hasn't been easy for me. When there were challenges by some of these groups, it was always helpful to see the success in action. Whether it was feedback from my staff or face-to-face, appreciative conversations with a parent or a teacher, I always remembered why I was doing what I was doing. We don't need to remember our why; the reality is WE as leaders are under attack, and we already know our whys. We need real practical strategies to control our reactions to the mess, not reminisce on our why.

I'm always appreciative and flattered reading glowing comments from our staff about the intentional way our leadership team tries to grow our culture every single day. But like my colleague who talked about the mess knows, it isn't all sunshine, rainbows, and trophies in schools. It's HARD! It's a MESS! It's defeating, and it can be gut wrenching as a leader. My messy colleague talks a lot about taking care of the people who are taking care of the kids. He's right – a great administrative team takes care of the teachers and staff because they are the ones leading our culture on the front lines, every single day.

But again, who is taking care of the ones supporting the ones taking care of the students? Who is there to help the administration when they are struggling? Who is there to help the Principal when a parent comes after them? And to top it off, who is there to help the Superintendent when they are drowning? Of course there is a chain of command for handling problems, but is there a chain of support that also moves up? We have to find time to be intentional, to be thankful for our educational leaders, for our Stressed Leaders who are constantly living in the mess. We have to find these positive moments because they are there; they just need to be acknowledged and recognized. We need to be intentional about sharing the positive moments so we can know our value, while fighting through the mess.

Living in the mess is simply what we do. But what happens when you live in the mess and don't realize exactly how the mess is impacting all of the other areas of your life? Your negative attitude from dealing with work problems bleeds into your relationship with your spouse, leads to outbursts with your children or frustration with your physical appearance. I lived in the mess for many years and am guilty of everything I just listed. Once I realized that the mess was controlling all components of my life, I started to find ways to slowly combat the mess. Simple solutions during my daily grind to no longer let the mess have its way with me was my promise to myself. For some people the grind of the mess never slowed them down, but that's not reality for everyone. For most, the ~~Stressed~~ Leaders movement exists to keep you in the game, to offer real solutions.

One of the first changes I made was a series of daily habits that were impacting the start to my day everyday. My morning routine heading off to work started the same way nearly every day for about twenty years:

- Head out the door to work, carefully loading strategic music to get me in the mood for a great day. Music is essential to my daily grind and output, and I have always enjoyed shuffling my tunes instead of listening to the radio.
- On my way to work, I would stop for a donut or two and a large soft drink or sweet tea. It just became a daily habit.
- Then, I would arrive at work, sit down in my chair, and immediately start checking emails, responding to the latest fires that would present themselves. I would start each day binging sugar and responding to one crisis after another that would frustrate me. While responding amidst each crisis, the angry parent email would appear, the disgruntled paraprofessional would request a union meeting, and a simple memo communication from a secretary would have a passive-aggressive tone. The death by one thousand pinpricks would continue, all while handling real crises. It was no wonder my mood became edgy, frustrated, stressed, and combative.

To counter all of this, I eliminated these poor habits and replaced them with superior habits. The first thing I do every morning now is hit the gym. Whether it's a prescribed lifting session, a morning run, a weighted ruck, whatever it may be, it gets my mind in the best possible sense of accomplishment and motivation to start each day with success. Then, I quit eating the sugary processed garbage. Not only am I getting healthier, but I also am eliminating more than five dollars in purchases each morning from my wallet. Finally, I quit checking emails first thing in the morning at the office, rather I find someone to speak to, something to do such as writing someone to express gratitude to that will start each day with joy.

I created the ~~Stressed~~ Leaders movement to work directly with the leaders who are drowning in the mess: those leaders who feel isolated, who need a shock to the system, who need to lead from the front but also know they need to lead from the rear, the leader who knows they can challenge themselves to do hard things and that huddling up with a community of fellow leaders will lead them to not drown in the mess but survive and dominate the mess. I created the movement to turn Stressed Leaders into ~~Stressed~~ Leaders.

1

~~stressed~~ LEADERS

SHOCK THE SYSTEM

Sitting poolside at the Longboat Key Members Club bar, I struck up a conversation with a sun-kissed widow who laughed at my jokes, our back and forth easy. The January Florida heat warmed my shoulders as I spent the afternoon storytelling with a lonely woman whose lived experiences would eclipse most people's. As she regaled me with her player stories of NBA front office experience, the flashbacks of my youth playing NBA Jam arcade games with a pocketful of quarters or watching CBS basketball games on Sunday afternoon winter TV – Detroit, Boston, Chicago rivalries, were pleasant memories amidst too many iced drinks.

On many family vacations, while my wife would lounge in a chair working on tanning her Irish-toned skin and my kids played in the pool, I would often be at the swim-up bar, swapping stories with my new-found friends. Back home it was thirty degrees and snowing, but here in Florida during Christmas break, the temperature was in the seventies, and I was finally able to let loose. As a Stressed Leader, I'd earned it, right?

For years, I had justified these vacations as a way for me to decompress and break away from the stress of a demanding leadership position, the always watchful public eye, and from my own desire to be the best, always-on-the-clock, servant leader. The kids stopped by from time to time to get virgin daiquiris and order some food, then meandered off to do their own things. I could have been spending quality time with my children, but instead, I succumbed to my own leisure, enjoying entertaining conversations, and imbibing in spirits at the bar.

In my mid-forties with so much at stake, bellied up to the swim-up bar, this was not a place of pride. With an incredible career as a superintendent of one of the best rural districts in Illinois and a man planning to help his fellow educational leaders de-stress their lives, I began to realize that the choices I was making while "de-stressing" did not match my mission or purpose.

I would listen to the horror stories of my colleagues, my friends, the people I care about deal with the stress of their districts, and I would quietly thank my stars that my situation was better, while I searched for advice to help them solve their problems. I would tell myself I was too blessed to be stressed. I dealt with stress better than anyone I knew. Who else was a superintendent, a part-time adjunct college professor, a writer, a planner of ~~Stressed~~ Leader retreats, a dad who coached his daughter's travel softball team, a man who made every effort everyday to work with his children at their sports, their studies, or to plan fun things to do as a family? Who else was a man writing books to de-stress late into the evenings, a man impervious to the powers of stress? Who else could handle my daily grind? Nobody, or so I thought. My overflowing plate was a source of pride. I was elite, right?

I felt like a fraud, an imposter. I was a victim of my own decisions and choices. I didn't say NO to anyone. I would put everyone else first, myself last, because that's what a servant leader is supposed to do, right? I was doing everything I could to please everyone else but also trying, and miserably failing, to lead from the front.

I never realized just how misguided this approach was until it was almost too late. I had put this career in front of my wife, my family, and my own health. Sure, I had gained weight, then lost it, and convinced myself that weight training and running were the only needed outlets to de-stress. But it wasn't enough to really move the needle. The regimen and workouts six days a week were just more items on the list to cross off. I told myself the beach getaway a couple of times a year was my excuse to let loose – to de-stress. I had earned that BECAUSE of my dedication to my job, and I was going to spoil my family and myself with an exotic trip to paradise. Until that January day at the Longboat Key VIP member bar when I realized there was more to my mission to truly move away from being a Stressed Leader.

Looking back, it is all so clear now, that I was deceiving myself about all of these events. I see now, in reflection, that I was lying to myself. I was overwhelmingly stressed to the point where subconsciously a vacation led to justifications for my behavior. I lied to myself, saying an extravagant vacation had been earned. While the stressors are problems in our lives, I find it is the justification of excuses that are even bigger problems. Mental justifications and rationalizations are like participation trophies. "I did this, so I get that," is a mentally weak framework to hold yourself to misguided standards. I was guilty of this for years. I would run miles… then go eat fried chicken. A 5:00 AM workout… meant I'd earned a Steve's Bakery donut. Three straight months of dedicated fitness and career success meant I had earned a vacation… where I deserved to let loose. However, when we justify behaviors or actions that are below our standard of excellence, we never learn resilience because we default to comfort.

I had succumbed to a way of managing the stress I didn't think I had. I was unfocused. I had become distracted from what mattered. They say the Devil works in distractions, removing our focus from where it needs to be. Keeping me distracted was working to advance my career but hurting my relationships. How could I let this happen? How could I trick myself for so long about who I was as a leader, as a father, and as a husband? This self-realization was earth shattering, mind-blowing, and defeating. But some believe that out of the Devil's destruction, God offers a solution. Perhaps this day was the window into what I needed to do. I needed space. I needed to re-evaluate my focus and find a better way. I needed to SHOCK MY SYSTEM.

Why do you need to shock the system? You need change. You've consumed yourself with the work when, the reality is, this job will be there even if you aren't. They will advertise your job posting before they write your obituary. You must have boundaries, if you don't, your performance will suffer at work and, more importantly, at home.

Here's why you currently fail: you have sacrificed your *don'ts* (your list of unflinchables, your boundaries). Immense willpower is needed to create space and disconnect from stressors. However, it takes time to make significant changes. Even if that change begins at just five minutes a day, do it; make the change. JUST START!

YOUR DON'TS:

✓ Don't be obsessed with your phone, checking emails at home, sending messages to staff at all hours about "critical" items, mindlessly scrolling social media sites when you should be present at home. Put the phone down. Disconnect!

- Whether it is the needy parent, the disgruntled staff member, or the concerned student, they email, text, or message you at night and expect you to respond. Why do they lack such barriers? Is it technology's convenience? Is it a lack of appreciation of privacy in an always on-call digital age? No. They send such messages BECAUSE YOU RESPOND! Your actions have become a poor workplace habit, and now, it has become the expectation. You have allowed the barriers to no longer exist. What boundaries are there if you are always *ON?*

- Don't kid yourself and say, "If I don't respond now to these super important emails and messages and update my twitter now, when will I do it? If I disconnect from my phone at night, I'll have to get to work at 5:00 AM to get something done!" The truth is, those meaningless emails will always be there; they'll keep coming in. How many times have you unsubscribed from email lists, just to have ten to fifteen more the next day? If you are like me and can't stand unread emails, find ways to make space such as scheduling time on your calendar to read and respond to emails or turning off your notifications at strategic times so unread emails are not weighing on your mind.

✓ Don't be a Marine- You DON'T have to be the first one in, last one out. You don't have to be there before everyone gets there. I used to chase the sunrise to get to work. There's nothing better in the winter in Illinois than getting to work in the dark and leaving in the dark, right?

- BE THERE - when you are there, BE THERE, FULLY, MENTALLY, AWAKE, AWARE, ENGAGED. What are your critical attention focused needs: an angry parent's email about the dress code? C'mon! Is your critical energy needed for a response to a teacher's supply purchasing request? Is your maintenance director's email about bleacher inspections paramount for your day's success? How about a nighttime custodian's note about a teacher's classroom messes? No, those will all be there when you get to work. While these are all routine tasks, you need to remove yourself from such trivial distractions at home. Make space, remove yourself from your phone. Later in the book, we will talk about your "On" and how you handle yourself when you are On.

- Early in my administrative career, I was home but NOT home. I would be continuously doing things at home that could be done at school: checking emails, responding to emails, putting plans together, or lists for the following day. I wasn't there for my family. Eventually, the job became all I thought about, and I was consumed with the list of things to do. I would say "family first," but I wasn't modeling or practicing what I preached. I was doing everything I thought I needed to do as a district leader and being the help desk for everyone rather than being a great husband and father at night. Everyone needs a break. If you tell people the expectation is to work hard at school but also leave the work at school, you need to model what that looks like.

- ✓ Don't be a terrible listener. Boy do I struggle with listening! Since I was a kid, I have ALWAYS wanted to share my ideas. I would be present in a conversation, but I would be thinking about my ideas, my sparks, my plans, not really listening to my partner. It's *still* a problem for me. I see my twelve-year old son mimicking the same behavior and find myself coaching him (and laughing at myself). Be present; treat each conversation as an opportunity to learn. Close the laptop; put the cell phone away, and LISTEN. Don't try to control the conversation with your great ideas.
    - I've had to put my cell phone in my pocket, close my computer, and just make eye contact and listen. Listening actively means shutting the hell up. Don't try to immediately solve someone's problem; make them a part of the solution. Validate their situation, "I know you took time out of your day to share this with me, and I want to thank you for that. How can I help?" "What I hear you saying is…" What can be done to help the individual solve the problem or grow?
- ✓ BE HELPFUL, BUT DON'T BE THE HELP DESK. Learn to delegate. Just because it's easier for you to do it rather than communicate how you want it done, don't keep it all inside. I struggle with this. I struggle to trust someone to do the work because I envision it my way. As it turns out, the better I have become at this, the better the end product becomes because I've surrounded myself with better people than me. Empower your people to lead and take chances. Being the help desk leads to:
    - Burn out: you are taking on everyone's problems and trying to fix them as if they were your own. Don't dip into

your email inbox to start your day. You will be in the wrong mindset to help people throughout the day because you are dealing with other people's problems.

- If you are always fixing or always doing things for other people, they have no ownership of the process. Delegation is giving responsibility to someone. Every voice matters right? Document the successes and strengths of your people, and empower them to solve their own problems. "What do you need to solve this problem, and how can I help?" Keep the ownership with the individual; don't be the help desk. LISTEN – ACTUALLY, LISTEN. Then, follow up after so they know they were heard.

Be intentional with your plans. At night, close the laptop. Just because you are home, doesn't mean you are home for your spouse and children. Be present, but be intentional with WHY you are present. The job will be there long after you retire, quit, or are asked to resign. So, focus on the job that matters – your role as a leader in your home. Shock the system by saying:

I WILL...
- ✓ Put my phone away and NOT respond to work emails, texts, messages, needs.
- ✓ Listen attentively with intention to my spouse and kids.
- ✓ Help a colleague with a problem they have shared with me, not solve it for them but empower them to do so.

At the end of the day, you can fail at work, but do you really want to fail at home? My wife and two children mean everything to me. If I fail them, I've failed at life.

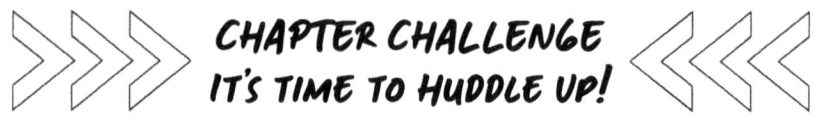

CHAPTER CHALLENGE
IT'S TIME TO HUDDLE UP!

How can you shock your system from its current state of drowning? Plunging into my first ice bath was a physical shock to my system, but as I quickly discovered, the benefits of cold therapy was a mental shock as well. It allows your body to open up, releasing tension and toxins, moving us away from being Stressed Leaders. At our first ~~Stressed~~ Leaders Retreat, dozens of first time ice bathers took the plunge, some hesitantly, and immediately felt the benefits I knew they would receive. By plunging under the frozen surface, your inhibitions relax and your brain fog quickly filters away. What is *your* shock to the system?

What actions can you take right now to shock your system? Are you preparing to be counted upon in a moment of crisis? Resilience is a big factor in this preparedness. The keys to resilience are hard work, failing, and actions that shock your system, challenge your bad habits, and attack those justifications. The opposite of resilience is doing nothing, opting out, or continuing down a path of regret. How do you shock your system? Maybe it's a long-range goal that seems insurmountable or deeply challenging. One of my long-range, monumental goals as an early forty-something was to bench press 300 pounds, something that seemed impossible at the outset of my health journey.

Maybe strength training isn't your shock to the system, but perhaps there is something deeper in your life holding you back from true success. There will be something that pulls at you, that thing you know you are supposed to do, but a barrier is standing in your way, and you may refuse to admit that. I had lied to myself for years when it came to my physical appearance. "I don't look that fat. I carry the weight well." Lies – just plain lies. You are your thoughts. You own them, and they become the truth in your head, whether they are right or wrong. I had convinced myself for far too long that these lies were, in fact, true.

Consumption was my roadblock. The wrong foods, the wrong stress relief, the wrong thoughts were consuming my body and mind. While I have always enjoyed running and strength training, nutrition is an area I have hidden from. It's the uncomfortable internal conversation I knew I needed to have but buried and ignored. The justifications of *I've earned this chocolate, I deserve to binge-watch Netflix on a rest day* are mental barriers we create for ourselves. Your thoughts are the biggest obstacles in the way of achieving that shock. When I had trained for more than a year and was getting seriously stronger, I came to realize there was something else missing. I needed to shock my system and admit to myself that my eating habits were holding me back. You can't out train a bad diet.

Working out has never been a struggle for me, but controlling my eating habits has always been a challenge. Shocking my system was attacking my gut, NOT working on my bench press. Working on the bench was more fun and more immediately gratifying, but the long-term habit loop necessary to really improve was the diet. My ability to prepare for a moment when clutch is needed required me to not stop at a gas station for a donut or not grab a bite size candy bar from the main office. Everyone's shock to their system is different, but remember your goals, and ask yourself a simple question: Am I making the daily sacrifice to get what I want?

My challenge for you: Shock your system; take the actionable steps now to make a change to your journey. Set a long-range goal, but set measurable micro goals to achieve your grand goal. Hold yourself accountable, and shock yourself with the changes. To truly shock your system, you must become resilient. Resiliency cannot be bought, and you cannot luck into it; it must be earned through hard work, losses, and mindfulness. Most importantly, be faithful. Before you quit, know that the greatest blessings come from your ability to stay.

2
~~stressed~~ LEADERS
60 FIRST

"You can't pour from an empty cup." How many times have you heard this crutch of a statement? We are leaders, our cup is always running empty. Enough excuses about how serving others keeps us running on empty. As leaders, within our homes and our organizations, we often take immense pride in our ability to serve others. We will dive deep into servant leadership later, but the old mantra is what we do. Embrace it. You've become a Stressed Leader because you do attempt to pour from that empty cup. You attempt to get the last possible drop out of your system every single time and the results may be good temporarily but will lead to terrible long-term results. It's also the honest reality; you MUST pour from this cup to be an effective leader. It is also toxic to blame your leadership for emptying this cup. You control your cup, and your need to fill that cup is your responsibility. As leaders, we often suffer from imposter syndrome and will allow outside noise to dictate our perceptions. Other people's doubts or limitations upon you are not your limitations.

For years I showed up early to work to put the time in, to prepare for the day, the next week, then I taught all day and coached all night until it was time to head home after the game. Earlier I told you about my poor morning routines at the gas station before and after work – a quick pit stop for a couple greasy slices of pizza, a forty-eight ounce fountain soda, and maybe some chocolate chip cookies to top it all off. I did that for years until I realized it was killing me. But it was easy; it was comfortable. I knew it was killing me but lacked the conscious willpower to do anything about it.

We have to put ourselves first, as leaders, so we may serve others. We have to admit that the failures we allow ourselves to make are not sacrifices for others but penalties against ourselves. Put yourself first; there are simple fixes to accomplish this. Many of us work in a service based industry and spend much of our lives focusing on other people's well being. But ask yourself, why don't we care more for ourselves? Most of us on this journey have been or are leaders, coaches, and influential people. Scores of folks depend upon us to be better versions of ourselves. Once again, we serve others, and in the same vein, allow other people's limitations to become our own.

I wallowed for over twenty years in self-created misery because I refused to take care of myself first. As a former head coach of young athletes, then a coach of leaders, I put my coaching hat back on and created a playbook with rules and principles to put myself first and quit failing. Anyone can do this, but willpower and an honest self-assessment of why you allow yourself to fail is needed. Until you can conquer your own willingness to repeatedly fail and make excuses, these rules will be difficult to adhere to. But having a playbook in your hands and consistently adhering to it, will get you on the right path as a ~~Stressed~~ Leader who needs to go first.

RULE 1: ENOUGH EXCUSES, GET UP OFF THE MAT

It took me a long time to realize that making excuses and negotiating with myself was my biggest hurdle in this journey. The *I'll start tomorrow* rabbit hole would consume me. If I am starting tomorrow, then I can eat fried chicken for dinner with fries, a roll, and stop for a peanut buster parfait, right? The *I'm too sore and need a rest day* and other traps were always a mental negotiation where discipline and comfort collide. Quit negotiating with yourself! I had always been good at being committed for a couple of weeks in a fitness or diet journey but would fall off the wagon. I had to get myself through several mechanisms, like 75 Hard and my own iterations of challenges, before I finally realized it was always YOU vs. YOU. The ability to stop negotiating failures with myself and accepting them as blips in a progress journey was humbling. When I fell off the wagon, I would beat myself up, and before long, I was a few weeks off the journey stumbling back into bad habits. It wasn't until I refused to accept a zero, refused to negotiate with myself that I established consistency. Consistency isn't working out six days in a row, or three weeks consecutively, it is a daily grind that never ends – not today, not tomorrow, it's just what we do. You're going to have setbacks, you will have zeroes, but get up off the mat and refuse to take another one. Do not allow yourself to justify those setbacks or lapses. The credit is earned by the one who is actually in the arena, like President Roosevelt opined. The person in the arena strives valiantly, errs, and comes up short again and again. You did not earn that ice cream, rather your workout earned you a rest day with some light walking. Do NOT let that punch keep you down and let you fall off the consistency train. There is no effort without error. You get knocked down... that's fine, but don't let one punch cripple you. GET UP OFF THE MAT!

RULE 2: FIX YOUR POSTURE – MAKE A STAND

The way you present yourself to others matters. If you slouch, you look soft, lazy, and unconfident. If you stride effortlessly, chest out, chin up, eyes locked on the prize – people take notice. Like I tell my children: a warm smile, a firm handshake, and a straight back will take you a long way in life. Whether you want to accept it or not, we are all drawn to confidence. The way you stand says a lot about your fortitude. Slouching conveys defeat, low self-confidence, and demonstrates a lower status, which prompts others to treat you poorly and reinforces weakness. If you look good you feel good, right? Stand up straight, push your shoulders back, and elevate your chest. Make eye contact, shake a hand firmly, smile, and portray confidence to yourself and others. You'll feel better, show respect, and earn more respect. And there's nothing wrong with throwing on some crisp, clean, fancy clothes. Several days a week I dress to the nines at work. Some people judge; some question the intention. None of that matters, I know why I do it. I do not dress to impress others but to send a message about how I feel about myself: I will command your respect with actions but also my appearance. When someone says, "Hey you look like Spencer Strasmore lately with that suit," that's a compliment I'll stand up proudly for. Standing tall, especially in the face of adversity or tough times, speaks to your character and resilience. This is it – draw a line in the sand and tell yourself, NO MORE! No more slouching, no more looking soft, no more appearing timid, shy, or lacking confidence. Fixing your posture is more than just standing up straight, it sends a message about who you are and what you stand for.

RULE 3: LEARN TO BE A GREAT LISTENER

In chapter one I wrote about listening. Now, I reassert this critical point. In today's age of distractions and on the go everything, find space, slow down, and lean into a conversation with your spouse, your children, your parents, your colleagues. Listening is a critical piece of leadership. It will make you better as a leader, especially in your relationships. The people in your circle need your ear, they demand your attention, and they need a listening ear. In our relationships, we often distract ourselves with less important items, and sadly, in an era of information – even meaningless information – at your fingertips, listening is becoming a lost skill. Assume the person you are listening to might know something you don't. As a good listener, you can learn while helping others solve problems as well as genuinely show you care about someone or something.

A critical flaw of many leaders is negative self-talk. How you listen to yourself is a skill often overlooked. The enemy lies within. The adversary inside you talks poorly about you, celebrates your failures and missteps, creates roadblocks, challenges you to continue to fail. Resist the trap of your negative self-talk! Finding purpose within your hardship, resisting such a trap, listening to who you know you can become, and leaning into what has happened to you are powerful growth steps. If you can dial into ignoring your negative self-talk, finding the purpose within your hardship, doing the hard things you set out to conquer, and growing positive self-talk, eventually that enemy within will flee.

RULE 4: GET YOUR HOUSE IN ORDER
Setbacks and suffering are inevitable in life. Bad things and missteps will happen, but how you respond to those is the measure of your character. Don't lie to yourself and justify why these setbacks and your flawed response to them are OK. Some people respond with denial, helplessness, anger, or even acts of vengeance. You have to get your own house in order first. The definition of your house can mean many things to many people, but what does it mean to you? My house begins with my mind. I am my toughest critic at times and realizing, knowing, and admitting to that, I have to remember I'm just trying to get a little better every day, win each day. Next, my house extends out of my own head to my journey. My wife and kids take notice of my daily grind. They know I leave the house at 4:45 every morning to get a workout in, sometimes even on weekends. They know how hard I work in my career, and I want them to see this journey with clear eyes. To be healthy in this world today, especially as a busy leader, you have to do what others are not doing. I want my family to know that Dad is a grinder, his work ethic is unmatched, and he is not afraid of pain. But I also want them to know I'll drop anything to take them to the batting cages, to take my wife out to dinner with friends, to talk to my son about his favorite NFL wide

receiver, or to just watch a stupid movie together, play some euchre or Rummikub, and laugh together.

My family also knows my flaws and my struggles with poor dietary habits. As I used to tell my athletes, there is always someone watching. My children see me struggle with cravings and impulse. A friend once asked, "Are you a toddler?" when I was venting about my snacking impacting my fitness and diet. Do you cave to simple cravings like a toddler crying for a treat? People can be controlled by cravings to obtain comfort, uninspired to do something that may challenge that comfort. My family knows of my lack of patience, but as an accountability measure, I've talked with each one of them about my efforts to be better in all of these flaws – not only for the love they deserve but as an accountability they can help me with. A house out of order can be crippling, especially if you allow yourself to be buried in misery. But some people make peace with the chaos and devote themselves to clearing out the cobwebs and making a positive difference. Which type are you?

RULE 5: DON'T PLAY OTHER PEOPLE'S GAMES – IMPROVE YOURS

Don't score keep. Scorekeeping is one of the most dangerous games we play as adults. It is a sign of immaturity and insecurity. You may be jealous of Tom getting the promotion or the nice ride the Carson's pull up in, but your journey is yours, not theirs. When you wallow in comparisons of what you don't have, you fail to assess the good things you already have and avoid the focus of the journey you have chosen to undertake. It is vital to recognize your own excuses and talk down the mental blocks, the hurdles, the bad habits, your own BS. I say it often, but it's always YOU vs. YOU. You may think you are scorekeeping Tom, but in reality, you are scorekeeping your own insecurities. Improve your game; don't play someone else's. Don't try to keep up with the Joneses. You should be comparing yourself to where you were yesterday, not to where somebody else is now.

Amongst seven billion plus people, you will always find someone better than you at something. Likewise, you will also find people who will wake up every morning and continue to believe their own BS, who justify their own excuses and bad habits. While in the last chapter I coached you to shock your system, you also need to realize a lightning bolt moment is not going to magically change everything for you. You must rewire your bad habits, the justifications, that fear of pain. Instead, measure yourself against yesterday to be a progress-minded, goal-focused individual. Most of my mornings start like any other: a demanding lift and some hot coffee after my shower. However, one morning I woke up and told myself, when those boots hit the ground, the Devil is going to be scared. Instead of just going through my lift, I added a twenty pound ruck vest and for the next hour, ratcheted up the intensity and the pools of sweat I left behind. No prisoners, no zeroes, and just a little bit better today than I was the day before. To top it off, a couple of my accountability measures witnessed my actions and were there afterwards with a fist bump, a smile, and to shout me out on X. It's YOU vs. YOU, not you vs. your neighbor. There is only one winner or loser on your journey; either way it is going to be YOU. Take measure of your daily grinds and incremental growth. Celebrate your wins, play your game and grow your game.

RULE 6: WHO YOU SURROUND YOURSELF WITH MATTERS
Who you surround yourself with matters because you will become those people. Take a look at your inner circle. Objectively, what makes each one of them tick? Are they good people? Is their idea of a good time drinking while watching Sunday football all day? Are they the kind of people who whisper in corners, scorekeeping what everyone else has? Are they jealous? Are they people you can count on?

Or, are they the people you aspire to be like? Could you call one of those people your hero? Do the people in your inner circle take action to make YOU better? Are YOU acting to make each of THEM better? Surround yourself with people who will help you achieve your goals and support your beliefs. Surround yourself with people you want to be. As you start to make changes, do not be surprised if some of the people in your circle doubt you or tempt you into falling off the wagon and reverting back to making poor decisions. You will become the summation of who you surround yourself with. As you change for the better, keep your inner circle tight as an accountability check, and explain why you are making these changes. Your inner circle may change to include people online who may not be your best friends but WILL support your journey and hold you accountable for your successes and failures. They may even push you harder than those who mean the most to you. True family and friends will support your journey, but know that some may not because they are struggling and stressed out as well.

RULE 7: CARE FOR YOURSELF LIKE YOU WOULD CARE FOR A LOVED ONE

Imagine your child gets sick. You would meticulously follow the doctor's prescribed orders to get your little one healthy. You would be diligent and focused on the care, treatment, and medications they needed. But when *you* are struggling, do you follow a healthy prescription? Or do you miserably spend time in self-loathing? Don't get me wrong, I've had the man-flu a time or two, and it can be crippling. But in all seriousness, why don't we care for ourselves, sick or healthy, like we would for our spouse, our child, a loved one, or even a student? Heck – many of us take better care of our pets than we do ourselves.

At thirty-seven, I was headed in for an SVT ablation surgery inside my heart. I was 365 pounds – my high water mark. In terms of physical condition I was fat and felt like a pathetic excuse for a man. The doctor tried to assure me that this condition was simply electrically related to my heart. I asked if my weight was a factor. He looked at me quizzically, as if to say, "Yeah, Bud. Push away from the table a time or two will ya!" I read it on his face as in true doctor speak he gave me the, "Well, yes. You might want to watch your diet and exercise regularly." I was far too young to be dealing with major medical surgeries and needed to do something about it. How could I let myself get to this horrific point, lying helpless in a hospital bed with two small children and a wife looking on nervously? I needed to focus on myself. For twenty years, I put my life on hold, focusing on the immediate needs of my wife and kids, my students, my athletes, my career, and all the while I made decision after decision that was crippling my body, my health, and my mind. I needed to take care of myself like I would take care of my children; I needed to GO FIRST!

RULE 8: APPRECIATE YOUR BLESSINGS
Everyone reading this book has bountiful blessings to appreciate. We are leaders who have earned respect and blessings. Yet amidst the grind of our careers, of chasing success at all costs, how often do we sit back and truly appreciate our blessings? Oftentimes, we appreciate the moments when they are too late. We reflect on the passing of our loved ones; we commemorate the relationships that suffered after they were lost. We chew internally on the words unsaid. Suffering is inevitable, and some people just seem to have a worse lot in life than others. We've all been dealt a hand that seems unfair at times, but rather than appreciate the good, we dwell on the bad.

A great mentor of mine, Mr. Doug Evans, once told me and would preach to the teams he coached, "You're never as great as when things are going good, and you're never as terrible as when things are going bad." That perspective is important to remember when we are struggling. It's also paramount to remember all the good in our lives. My wife is loved by many because she is one who shows and shares her appreciation for others. She makes people feel loved. While sometimes I can be too focused on chasing life's conquests, I sit back and regard how great she is at slowing down and appreciating the day, appreciating her family, and her blessings. She is constantly living passionately, in the moment, undistracted, oftentimes for others, because she truly cares about everyone else.

RULE 9: FOCUS ON A HIGHER PURPOSE – NOT INSTANT GRATIFICATION

We can use suffering as an excuse to live carelessly in the moment, or we can do something meaningful to minimize the suffering. I messed up my diet, so I'm going to allow myself one mistake, which leads to two, and then three, and so on. Instead of slipping down this awful slope of gluttony, stop, find space, and ask yourself if this action is in line with your goals? Does this decision further advance your goals, or does it negatively impact what you're trying to do?

Stopping yourself, finding the slimmest amount of honest reflection and space is critical as we struggle along this journey of putting ourselves first. For me, I MUST find the time to stop and ask these questions. I live a non-stop lifestyle of all-gas-and-no-brakes chaos with my career and family demands. I embrace the grind, but what put me over the top in this pursuit was simply slowing down intentionally to ask specific questions internally. What is my higher purpose? What is my North Star? What guides my mission to be better each day, to go first? I know this cheesecake would taste amazing right now, but does it help support my mission? What does greatness in my life look like? Am I paying the price right now to get what I want? I would love to eat this cheesecake, but I also want to look good with my shirt off on my boat. It's only one little piece; I can just workout longer after work, run an extra mile, add a few more sets, add another plate to the ruck vest. Again, the justification of poor decision-making was something that crippled me. I would get so fixated on pleasing myself that I had to step back, stop, think, and recognize I was acting like a toddler. A toddler throws a fit and reacts to basic impulse. Does this decision support what I say I want to become? We can all say the right things, but our actions speak of our real intention. I am not saying you should become a monk and never feed your impulse, but having an honest conversation, in the moment, to realize what you are doing and why will be a helpful practice. I control what I do, and having a focused and intentional daily routine keeps me on task with the chaotic demands of my purpose. Focus on your purpose in life, not instant gratification that may devalue your purpose to stay comfortable.

RULE 10: BE THE HERO OF YOUR OWN STORY

If your life was a movie, would you watch it? I can confidently say that although I've been blessed with a large amount of success, my life's movie would not have earned many followers in my 20's and 30's. While successful, with some great scenes, the whole production would not be epic. Instead of being a hero, I might be cast as an extra. I celebrated a hall of fame coaching career for sure, but that was more a product of the athletes who bought into our system and elevated themselves than it was following a hero. As a Stressed Leader, my story would have limped along the nice arc of a successful educator, but that doesn't sell tickets. Perhaps the story of a guy picking himself up out of the ditch, dusting off the mistakes of a couple decades, digging his fingers into the dirt as he pulls himself up – maybe that's a hit.

As leaders, we need to be the hero of our own story. Ask yourself if your life was a movie and it started right now, would you want to watch it? What would the hero of your life's movie do right now? Would they get up off the mat? Would they get themselves out of that ditch? If your answer is no or you are unsure, then your movie isn't worth tuning in.

Do whatever it takes for this movie to be epic. We define ourselves far too often by our past mistakes and failures. We look at our past and say, "Well, that was me..." Adapt. Overcome the setbacks and failures that ruined your movie. Through humility, defeat, and the right amount of grit, you begin the hero's journey. Your movie starts NOW! You are the ~~Stressed~~ Leader right now. You're the person who has learned from those failures, and you can choose to be the hero of your own movie.

Write down your goals. This simple action is the foundation for growth. For one friend of mine, it was simply to get out of bed every morning and move for five minutes. He set his shoes and his workout gear next to his bed every night to slowly make actionable steps to become his own hero. He went from walking five minutes a day, to running ultra marathons. He wrote down the things he wanted to improve. He created a non-negotiable willpower to slowly but surely build this growth from five-minute walks to getting a small amount better each day. He became a samurai of willpower over things he wouldn't tolerate from himself. He wrote down mistakes he made in the past that he never wanted to see himself do again. He became the hero of his own movie, and you can too. You have to take action. You have to build momentum. You have to build confidence with each good decision you make from here on out to be the hero. YOU can do it!

The ten rules in this playbook are aimed at taking a Stressed Leader from a leader who puts themselves last to focusing on leading first. We must put ourselves first to truly change. Within those rules, two key facets stand above the others: willpower and habits. Our habits, whether daily or within certain activities, are the number one thing propelling us forward AND holding us back.

We all have amazing habits, but we all also have habits that are our kryptonite. Our beneficial habits are what lead to:

- The amazing connections we have within our relationships.
- The successful career that has led us to the top of our industry.
- Our ability to lead a team, to work a room, to close a sale, to accomplish a goal that we wrote down.
- Our best accomplishments.

Debilitating habits can hold us back as we fall into our old ways. This can be the reason we experience:

- Connections that aren't deep, leading to depression and frustration.
- Success but at a price, causing anxiety, worry, and fear of failure.
- Procrastination and celebrating only temporary wins.
- Feelings of failure and resentment, lying to yourself to celebrate minor wins.
- A problem you have not solved or a goal you failed to accomplish.

In essence, our habits are the predictor of our own success or failure with everything we do. Unfortunately, when we are failing it is because not only are our habits substandard, but we are continuously roaming through a habit loop of failures. The habit loop is well documented and is essentially a route we take to achieve outcomes, whether intentional or unintentional. In my experiences, the unintended habits consumed my progress and overpowered my wins within my habit loop. Cues become triggers to practice routines that can be successful or fail, and that success or failure will result in a reward or a loss.

CUE → ROUTINE → REWARD

Example from my life:
- Cue: Something at work doesn't go right for me and results in feelings of frustration or being overwhelmed by a frantic situation that demands my attention.
- Routine: I will drop other projects or important tasks in an effort to put this fire out. At times, I am guilty of becoming a prisoner of the moment.
- Reward: I will solve the problem resulting in a feeling of accomplishment or be forced to push forward, down this elaborate rabbit hole and not complete the other items I needed to complete in my day, leading to feelings of angst.

Cues like this can elevate my stress. The routine can lead me down several paths, some resulting in rewards and some that result in more frustrating work. I feel more overwhelmed as I didn't achieve everything I had planned for that day. This can create a dangerous cycle of frustration when one does not complete tasks necessary to consider the day a win.

How do we resolve these internal conflicts? When thrust inside a fire, the usual response is to become a prisoner of the moment. Like a quarterback trying to navigate a final-quarter, two-minute, game-winning drill, we become obsessed with immediate decision making needed to address a situation. A cue has thrust us into the fire where our routine has been interrupted. Our snap decision could lead to a reward or punishment. The practical solution is the two-minute drill: Will this matter in two minutes? Will this matter in two hours? What about two days or even two months? Do these decisions matter right now, or can this wait?

We must first identify that the situation has the potential to elicit a habit loop that can take us down a bad path. Finding space and time to relax and consider multiple consequences and outcomes becomes critical in our response management. It is easier said than done to not become a victim or a prisoner of the moment. Before any actions can take place, we must identify what is currently going on. From there, we create a new plan of action for a better strategy on handling our habits. Willpower and self-awareness become musts to realize our own limitations and shortcomings.

After we have identified our shortcomings and our cues that could elicit poor responses, we must find space, then respond appropriately. For me, habit stacking became key to success when I got stuck after an initial win. I lost over one hundred pounds in my weight loss journey, but I also responded adversely to stressful situations. I had to pivot from looking at wellness to looking at my well-being. There were situations of my own making in which I would force myself into a backwards slide. Whether it was a tough weekend after a successful work week of workout and diet dominance or even just procrastination on tasks I didn't want to do, I had to address my own willpower.

Procrastination dies when you say JUST START! Just start, and once you get a few minutes into the workout or have a water in between drinks, the remainder of the action becomes easy. There are one thousand four hundred and forty minutes in a day, how are you capitalizing on those? You can fight procrastination the same way you fight poor habit loops – just start. Day-to-day motivations can change, but when you reassess your priorities and habits, your willpower builds. Motivation can be fleeting, but disciplined habits last. The first rule of willpower is to know thyself. You have to be able to look in the mirror and have an honest conversation with yourself.

You have to have self-awareness to have self-control. I didn't realize I was using alcohol as a stress reliever in my leadership journey. While drastically cutting back, it would still reappear in an uglier fashion. Know thyself: does alcohol serve your purpose? Or does it get in the way? Does it impact the momentum you are building? Are you associating alcohol with celebrations? I had to get to know myself. I haven't abandoned alcohol, but I do realize the answer to the previous questions is it does not serve my purpose, and it does get in the way. I also know it impacts my momentum. I have limited my alcohol consumption because I am my sharpest man when I'm sober. As I have lost a large amount of weight, I know that I can no longer manage sobriety with alcohol. I know that I'm better at my training when I'm not hungover. I know that the next day, I'm better at my mission when I'm not distracted. To go from habits, to controlling your willpower, you have to tell yourself YES! If you want to develop willpower, learn how to say yes to yourself, not what you won't do. Instead, say YES to those questions above. I know the answers to those questions, so instead I say that I will.

My **I WILL** statements include:

- ✓ **I WILL** set a date on the calendar by signing up for a race and completing it. *5K → 10K → ½ Marathon → ½ Ironman*
- ✓ **I WILL** eat this food because it's going to define my day positively and is an action towards my goals. *Two meals a day diet: heavy in protein, light in processed foods, sporadic yet calculated fasts inserted.*
- ✓ **I WILL** stop stressing about something and instead make space to assess my reactions to a situation. Utilizing my two-minute drill becomes key to my response to situations that could spark cues which lead to poor habit loops.

In all of my years as a student and then as a professor guiding other administrators, I voiced my frustration with theories. I would become frustrated with professors who never actually taught in a high school classroom, supervised the day-to-day events of a school, or led a school district. Theory has its place, but practical solutions were what I yearned for in my leadership preparation. Later, as I became a professor advising future educational leaders, I told myself I would always show real strategies and practical solutions for the complexity of educational leadership. So, how does a Stressed Leader lead first when they've mastered the playbook but the stress continues to build and they still feel like they are drowning? You need fast-acting stress relief strategies that can be of real help in the moment of stress, real solutions you can implement on the fly.

There are a number of helpful techniques, such as deep breathing and meditation, which can be fast-acting tools you can do anywhere or at any time. Whether you're about to be interviewed for your next leadership job or you're feeling overwhelmed by a difficult conversation you need to have with a colleague, it's important to have some stress reduction tools that can lower your stress immediately.

The best short-term strategies can be performed anywhere, take very little practice to master, are free, and provide instant relief. Here are four real, in the moment, practical solutions to keep you thriving in a difficult and stressful situation.

- **GUIDED IMAGERY** is like taking a short mental vacation. For me, I think of my many trips to Mexico. I picture idly sitting by the pool, basking in the warm sun with the ocean waves in the background, and a good book in my hand, relaxing early in the morning while the resort sits quiet. Some people use recorded cues like an audio clip or a mental go-to phrase to refocus. Once you know how to do it yourself, you can practice guided imagery on your own. Try it now. Close your eyes for a short moment, and walk yourself through your scene of peace. Think about all the sensory moments, those feelings of calm you engage in, and allow yourself to feel like you're really there. After a few minutes, open your eyes and return to the present moment, ready to act.
- **MEDITATION** brings short-term stress relief as well as lasting stress management benefits. There are many different forms of meditation to try – each one is unique and brings its own appeal. You might develop a mantra you repeat in your mind as you take slow deep breaths, or you might take a few minutes to practice mindfulness, which involves being in the moment. Simply pay attention to what you see, hear, taste, touch, and smell. When you're focused on the here-and-now, you won't be able to ruminate about something that already happened, and you can't worry about something in the future. Meditation and mindfulness take practice, but it can make a big difference in your overall stress level as it brings you back to the present.
- **FOCUS ON BREATHING** can make a big difference to your overall stress level. Breathing techniques can calm your body

and your brain in just a few minutes. The Wim Hof breathing technique allows me to slow down and find peace, lowering my heart rate, especially in stressful moments. This technique involves a series of deep, rapid breaths followed by holding the breath. The benefit is elevated oxygen levels and a calmed nervous system. The best news about these techniques is that no one around you will know you're doing them. So, whether you're in a stressful meeting or you're sitting in a crowded room, breathing exercises could be key to reducing your stress. While there are many different breathing exercises, one simple exercise includes breathing in through your nose and watching your belly fill with air. Count slowly to three as you inhale. Hold for one second, then slowly breathe out through your nose as you count to three again. Another exercise is to breathe in through your nose and imagine you're inhaling peaceful, calm air. Picture that air spreading throughout your body. As you exhale, feel yourself breathing out stress and tension.

- **TAKE A WALK** Exercise is a fantastic stress reliever that can work in minutes. At times I can become stressed with dietary decisions or social temptations. Simply taking a walk allows me to enjoy a change of scenery, which can put me in a different frame of mind and brings the benefits of exercise as well. For me, that walk allows me to digest my food a little more or slow down in a social setting that might push me into cues of poor decision making. Whether you just need to take a stroll around the office to get a break from a frustrating task or you decide to go for a long walk in the park after work, walking is a simple but effective way to rejuvenate your mind and body.

When I think of a good leader, I think of someone who is a servant, who puts others' needs ahead of their own. I've been fortunate to know many great leaders and am surrounded by several in my school district. BUT if we are truly leading others, we have to put ourselves first, right? I encourage you to put yourself first, to take care of yourself. In the past, I did not follow this advice. Even as I grew in my journey of improvement, I focused on organizational wins and my employees' victories, while putting myself last and NOT taking care of myself. I didn't prioritize myself, and for twenty years, I suffered because of it. I was always going last, and it led to a slippery slope of excuse making.

I truly am a workaholic. Ask yourself some simple questions about your work, and it might make sense why you do not choose to put yourself first. Self-assessing or reflecting on these questions might just bring you to a point of levity that you otherwise may have never considered. You may realize that despite your ability to follow a playbook, manage your stress, and create better habits, your career might just be the thing that is crippling all of the momentum you are trying to build. Are you a workaholic?

Workaholism Diagnosis:
1. Do you usually spend your idle time in work activities?
2. Do you usually think about work when not working?
3. Do you work well beyond what is required of you?
4. Do you fail to reserve part of your energy for your loved ones after work and stop working only when you are a shell of a human being?
5. Does it make you anxious and unhappy when someone such as your spouse suggests you take time away from work for activities with loved ones, even when nothing in your work is unusually pressing?

Maybe your workaholism is because you are a **success addict**:
1. Do you define your self-worth in terms of your job title or professional position?
2. Do you quantify your own success in terms of money, power, or prestige?
3. Do you fail to see clearly what comes after your professional successes?

4. Do you dream about being remembered for your professional successes?

When I first read the diagnosis of workaholics, I answered yes to each of the five questions. Sickening, isn't it? Then, I took the second quiz on being a success addict and yep, nailed all those too. Many people who suffer from workaholism show the same patterns of behavior as alcoholics. I know I have some addictive character traits. Because of this, I had to make some changes. I started forcing myself to go first. Making a commitment to my weight lifting, training, and eating better was critical to putting myself first.

I find myself somewhere between workaholic, addicted to success, and the gray man. The gray man is unable to leave his tortured mind unattended during his crushing schedule. He becomes so consumed that he loses his purpose, becoming lukewarm, drifting, and waiting for success, rather than striving for it. He no longer carries the banner of success, leading others behind him. Return to your passions by leading yourself first.

We love the image of ourselves as successful, not ourselves in true life. But you are not your job, and I am not mine. Do you say *My work is my life* or feel it is at least a source of your identity? I have said that my entire career; the school is part of my family and used to take great pride in this statement. But what does greatness look like in my life? Am I paying the price to get what I want? Sitting on my desk is a simple photo of my family and my goals. I urge you to create an identity statement and revisit it daily: Who are you? What are you about? Why are you here? You already know your why, you just have to hone it. Wake up everyday like it's the first day of your journey to go first! ~~STRESSED~~ LEADERS NEED TO GO FIRST.

Chapter Challenge
It's Time to Huddle Up!

In Chapter One we talked about shocking your system. Now it's time to take the next step, to evolve from being someone drowning in the mess, to strengthening your mind and achieving the level of greatness you haven't seen in some time. Shocking your system to jumpstart your journey towards a goal is critical to just getting started. A friend of mine, Dan Cox, a District Superintendent who has led keynote speaking sessions for the ~~Stressed~~ Leaders Retreat once told me that his journey started daily with just five-minute walks outside. Simple, measurable, achievable, realistic, and time-based, a SMART goal. But walking five minutes at first was a challenge. He needed to take down the little man on his shoulder who was full of doubt. Once you plant that seed of doubt in your mind, it is very easy to water that seed, developing it into an uncontrollable weed and a head full of doubts. If you are watering that seed with negative self-talk, you are NOT preparing yourself for a moment of clutch.

~~Stressed~~ Leaders need to go first, we need to toughen our mind, to not only kill that weed of doubt but pull the roots out and never allow it to return. To enhance my mind, I needed competition. I have always thrived on people doubting me, people questioning my abilities, physical or mental. While most of that was internalized, it was a trigger to motivate me to develop a calloused mind and to be mentally combative with the person across from me, in the gym. There is an importance in loving everyone who is in the gym working on their own journey, but whether it was the guy interrupting my work in the squat rack or the lady dying on a stair climber, these folks, unknowingly, were competing against me. Stepping back from this, I can see how it might seem slightly insane to think this way, but it motivated me, especially at the beginning of my journey. I can laugh about it now, but I would look across the gym at a woman walking on a treadmill and say to myself, "Not today, Ruthie. I'm taking this lift from you. I'm outworking you on the stair climber. I'm taking your soul!"

I learned this from a legendary endurance athlete, and it became my motivation to outwork everyone in the gym, no matter who they were or what they were doing. I was going first; I was putting my needs ahead of everyone. I was overcoming obstacles daily, all the while motivating myself through competition. When competition wasn't enough, I would focus on being the hero of my story.

While the journey is nowhere near done, my mental focus is that of something I am chasing: a healthy man with simple goals, to be proud of how I look and feel, an example for my family. Every workout is another step towards that goal.

I committed myself to getting help and support in a few different places that a couple of years ago, I would have been afraid to visit. First, I challenged myself to step out of my comfort zone by attending a game-changing personal conference. I had watched these guys doing amazing things with strength training and hybrid ironman training. The energy when they came together online represented something I had missed, that of a focused team, chasing a common goal.

Second, I told myself I would religiously wake up at 4:45 AM to workout prior to work every day. Conquering the day in the morning feels so empowering. It sets everything in motion, but there are struggles. A quick getaway to Vegas or a two-day work conference out of town stacked up some losses and forced me to reset myself back to a level of commitment that, unfortunately, I was slowly starting to let slide. A couple of days in a two-week stretch, turned into two days in a row. I finally held myself accountable and said ENOUGH! One simple decision before 5:00 AM sets in motion a series of victories or losses. When the comfort of your warm bed meets the mental discipline that demands your attention in the gym, that crossroads will define your next move, your day, your victories and defeats, and ultimately your journey.

Putting off until tomorrow what I could be doing right now used to be a giant barrier for me. I would tell myself *I'll start tomorrow.* Then, I'd go hard and be committed for a week or so but revert back to old ways. I finally realized at forty-two years of age that I needed to find a new challenge. I've always enjoyed running outside with some headphones and a great playlist. I like a good workout in the gym, but I still ate like a twenty-one-year-old college student. Many times I would say, *I just killed the gym, now I can eat half of a fried chicken. I just ran four miles – why not eat six chocolate chip cookies?* I also wasn't consistent with any type of training. One year, from August to May, I challenged myself to workout consistently, and I did but without much vision. The results: I did lose a good amount of weight, but I needed a new challenge to get over a staggering hump – the one hundred pound weight loss hump. Don't get me wrong, one hundred pounds is incredible! But I would simply stumble through workouts and eat inconsistently – one week I'd lose three pounds, but the next week, I'd gain it all back.

I was stuck at 265 pounds for months. A lot of people might have never guessed I had weighed 365 pounds. I would trick myself and say, *I carry it well.* Now, I look back at those old pictures and realize the amount of lost time, lost energy, and lost memories stacked up over twenty years. It hurts to admit that, but now, I'm razor focused on stacking wins, being a little bit better each day, and getting over that hump. I was seeking little things that a fat guy hadn't seen since his prior athletic days. It wasn't too much to ask – defined arms, some pecs that weren't man boobs, and that dang spare tire to be gone. I didn't need a six-pack, I just didn't want a trailer tire around my belt line.

Dates on a calendar were great springboards in my initial journey. However, the ultimate goal was I simply wanted to be confident in my appearance and set the tone for my family. I felt more confident, but I needed a push. How did I get from 270 to 235, over that hurdle I couldn't achieve?

I knew I needed a spark. I started following a young guy on Twitter for a while, along with a few other people to see who had an option that seemed to work for me. I didn't want some guy selling a lose-weight-fast diet; I wanted someone committed to helping me and committed to shoot me straight. When I finally met Mike in person, I realized his energy and accountability through community was exactly what I needed. His vibe matched my personality and needs, and I finally admitted I needed some support. Mike's online community gave me so much more than the push I needed. The community of guys in our group, pushing each other, cheering each other on, and holding each other accountable, especially when we lose, is more powerful than just a workout plan, a diet, or a training regimen. This group has given me the trust and accountability to push, to be pushed, to compete, and to trust in others to help me improve. I wouldn't have gotten over that hurdle without Mike's group. His "Best Day Ever" mantra is something I have carried over into my workplace, my personal life, and the way I have been attacking my workouts. I destroyed the workouts. I ate healthy meals, and developed habits that looped over and over daily until they simply became what I did. I put dates of competitions on the calendar, competitions with myself and competitions such as marathons and lifting challenges, ME vs. ME.

As I reflect on these lost memories in old pictures, it's easy to get frustrated, but the future with my wife and kids means too much to me to be upset. I won't start tomorrow because I'm living every moment, getting 100 extra jump shots in with my son in the gym, rebounding and running after each shot, right after my long workout. I get home and throw some passes to him. He thinks he's the next NFL or NBA superstar – who am I to question him? Then, a healthy meal of rice and chicken we all enjoy around our fireplace – those are the habits I can be proud of. I reflect on these images, and I see a different me, a different man, a different father, and a different husband. No more lost time, energy, or memories, and no more losses!

My challenge for you: Commit to yourself, and GO FIRST!

3

~~stressed~~ LEADERS
SERVE OTHERS

There's nothing quite like the glow off the glistening grass of a Friday Night Lights on small town football fields. One year, I was blessed to watch the journey of a group of young men on the football field as they traversed a championship season. I was on the sidelines watching these young men fight for a championship, one that would be inches from their grip only to be taken away in overtime of the quarterfinals playoff game. Our boys had the game in hand, only to see it escape their struggling grip at the last seconds. It was a tragic loss, one that many of the players still struggled with months later as their victor was crowned the eventual state champion. Yet the impact their coach had on his student's lives was his greatest coaching victory.

Our head football coach was relatively young in his head coaching journey, but he had been coaching for almost two decades. He was an inspiring man, a teacher of science, football, track and field, a leader of Christian Athletes, and an inspirer of young men. You wouldn't see him with popping veins in his forehead, screaming out motivational words through spit and grinding teeth, rather you would see him stoic, composed, and convicted on the sidelines, sometimes even with a big smile on his face.

Every Wednesday night, the coach guided his men in voluntary leadership seminars. What a great blessing for him to devote more of his time to raising not simply football players but future men, future fathers, and future husbands into what is a vital resource in America – compassionate, male leadership. I saw their impact as leaders in our school, in our community, and with the young boys who strove to be like them some day. They were growing as young men and learning valuable lessons on serving others.

I was not a coach or parent, but I felt like a part of the team, as an administrator, as a fan, and as a distant leader who cherished watching the team's leader. I learned a lot just observing him and his team that season. They held a book study each year, and I read along with them, not in their group but on my own. Each book I read brought me back to questions for my life: What values was I demonstrating for my wife and kids? What more could I do instead of sleeping through life?

Like many great leaders, their coach motivated me to be a better man, to put the tools in place for all teachers and coaches, so all of our students could have similar success and teachings. This coach, along with some concepts I adapted from a coaching chart in a book I read, *The Twin Thieves* by Steve Jones and Lucas Jadin, inspired me to create a list of things ~~Stressed~~ Leaders Do Better.

~~Stressed~~ Leaders ...

- **Serve Others** – Be a servant leader. Be someone who focuses on serving the people they have the privilege to lead. The needs of the team should outweigh the needs of the individual, celebrating the we over me. ~~Stressed~~ Leaders go last, putting the team above the individual.

- **Lead Themselves** – ~~Stressed~~ Leaders must lead themselves, as discussed in the last chapter. A ~~Stressed~~ Leader is a person of faith and conviction, and they lead themselves first, modeling the work consistently by doing the dirty work, having a growth mindset, and consistently living out the standards. Last chapter we spoke, at length, about going first. You know what you need to do as a ~~Stressed~~ Leader to go first.

- **Empower Others** – Give others ownership; allow their flair, their voice to be a critical part of the process. Some would question the celebration of individual flair in their persona, especially those without an ability to adapt to unique leadership needs. A ~~Stressed~~ Leader has found a way to get people to buy into the collective, while also allowing their expression and voice to be heard. As I reflect on empowering my own children, I see children daily who have been overprotected by loving parents who snow plow the road to keep it safe for those children at all costs. That snow plowing can lead to unsuccessful adults. Rather than overprotect them, let's give our children the tools to empower their resiliency. If we aren't speaking life into those we lead, then what are we doing?

- **Are the Buffalo** – Don't run from fear of failure or judgment. Rather run at them. The buffalo runs into the storm bravely instead of scattering without a plan, fleeing with reckless abandon. Effective leadership means managing the storms that continuously arise. We've all been there, but how we respond measures not only our effectiveness as a leader, but also our modeling of anticipated behaviors. Those who follow will see how their leader responds to these unique storms and adversity.

- **Deliver the Mail to the Right Address** – Provide direct feedback to the people who need to hear it the most. Put challenging issues on top of the table and have courageous conversations. When a fire rises, use the two-minute drill to remember that people are the heart and voice of our organization; sometimes, doing the hard thing is having the hardest conversation.
- **Shine Bright –** Shine a light on the behaviors you want to see by making celebration and recognition an essential part of your team's culture. When you recognize someone, then extend that recognition about the individual to someone else, it speaks volumes of your ability to celebrate your team's success. It is simple to tell someone they did a great job, but when you tell someone else how great Rich was in a time of adversity and that gets back to Rich from someone else, you've highlighted the greatness of Rich's actions.
- **Water the Bamboo, not the Weeds –** Success is not microwaveable; great leadership happens when you pour time into the hearts and minds of the people we serve. We have to reach them, before we can teach them. Bamboo takes years to grow underground, needing a lot of time and attention before it eventually shoots above the surface. On the other hand, if we water the weeds, they take a short amount of time to spring up. Focus your energy on the bamboo, not the weeds. Even watering your own weeds will force you into backwards momentum. We talked about that seed of doubt in your mind – don't spend time with negative self-talk or doubts, watering that weed in your brain.
- **Become Elite Listeners** – They don't care how much you know until they know how much you care. In each chapter, we have hit on the need to be a great listener. Get the point yet? ~~Stressed~~ Leaders listen more than they speak.
- **Embrace Change** – Change is inevitable, but growth is optional. ~~Stressed~~ Leaders are constantly emerging, evolving, and growing. Nobody likes change but a baby in a wet diaper. However, if we highlight change for growth opportunities not for just change's sake, we can improve the

organization and get collective buy-in when the growth is demonstrable.
- **Love Their Team –** The greatest counterpunch to fear is love. Bonds of love endure in a way bonds of fear never could. To care is to love. Sometimes, simply showing your team you care is all they need.

These ten leadership traits are all a part of a ~~Stressed~~ Leader going last and serving others with love. Leading with love is a concept all great leaders possess, but I have found that epic leaders show love at the most critical times, not just when things are going great. When the tenuous times test the greatest leaders, often, true colors will present themselves. Do you show genuine love for others' success?

Prior to being enshrined into the Hall of Fame as a coach, I always brought a message to our team each year about our journey, but the best thing I can say I ever did then as a coach and now as a leader, was to be mindful of mudita – being joyful for other people's success is one of the most rewarding feelings of quality leadership. I first heard about mudita from a former coach of mine. Extending the acknowledgement of someone else's success to others makes the feeling of gratitude even stronger. While a simple expression of congratulations for our football coach's success was extended in the moment, I found greater appreciation by showing him how impressed I was that he was asked to speak at coaching clinics and share the stories of love that his players and their parents told me about. Months later, during a scholarship interview for our Educational Foundation, one of his seniors explained in heartfelt gratitude what this coach did to help him turn his life around during football and the leadership sessions after the season ended. He showed he cared, that's it. Oftentimes, that is all our kids, our staff, our people truly need.

There are so many lessons one could take from that game, from that season, from that team. You never know when your competition is on the brink of collapse. The key is to just stay in the fight. No matter what happens, keep swinging. While they may have come up just short in that prizefight, those boys were still swinging a couple of weeks later on their basketball and wrestling teams. I knew their coach would keep swinging too, and as a leader of leaders, that was inspiring to see. It was a great pleasure of mine to see them swinging each Friday night. Sometimes, the end result of a great team is not a state championship like these boys deserved. But as they transitioned into basketball and wrestling seasons, they knew one man, their head coach was still there for them. It was also a great reminder that in times of strife and struggle, ~~Stressed~~ Leaders need to go last, to serve those around them. When I watched our coach walk off behind his team, I didn't have the words to share my appreciation, not of the great season or the record but of the way he led those young men with true mudita and love.

Leadership can be an isolating and lonely business. Kobe Bryant said, "If you're going to be a leader, you're not going to please everybody. You have to hold people accountable, even if you have that moment of being uncomfortable." ~~Stressed~~ Leaders cannot please everyone. It isn't about popularity; it is about your responsibility as a leader. It means making sacrifices for the betterment of the team, sometimes, at an individual's expense. It means having tenuous and tough conversations. It means making decisions that may not be popular and being willing to do what is right for the team, even if it means you won't be liked. You lead through your actions. You lead through the examples you set, how you interact with others, and how you create a standard for performance. When a ~~Stressed~~ Leader recognizes that leading the right way is not always the popular way, true organizational success can happen. Never let the critics, the masses, the chase of perfection, or the flawed expectations get in the way of serving others. For such success to occur, difficult conversations may need to happen that can often bring up hard feelings. Understanding that your decision-making might cause those you lead to dislike you, will allow your interpersonal relationships to grow. It takes more than a strong gut to lead and lead last; it takes leadership competencies for success.

My desire to lead comes from a passion for serving others. Far too often I have put myself last, but finding the balance between going first and going last is critical for a successful journey to becoming a ~~Stressed~~ Leader. A good leader must craft and hone leadership competencies such as the ones on the following list.

✓ **Build Relationships** – It starts with caring and connecting. To be an effective leader, you need to build relationships with people so you can establish trust and foster collaboration. People won't follow or listen until they know you and what you stand for. My coach's mudita for others built a foundation of trust; you must know them before you can teach them.

Then, you will grow, they will grow, and your love for their success will build a family of trust and success.
- ✓ **Create Accountability** – Leaders set and embody the standard. Accountability means taking ownership. Success doesn't happen without accountability. Creating accountability empowers you to ensure people take ownership of their actions. Watching a man build his vision for team success out of a loving familial concept where he empowers others was so meaningful to watch. Not only was he accountable, but through his leadership development in these players, their personal and team accountability allowed him to lead from behind, going last. Even in difficult times, that accountability piece of the players arose, where perhaps on other teams, the selfishness of the individual would have outweighed the success and accountability of all. These times create good conflict because it promotes responsibility and drives performance for success.
- ✓ **Communicate Effectively** – Effective leadership means effective communication. Communication is what you say, how you say it, and when you say it. The ability to pair strong relationships with effective communication is what drives change. Effective communication means articulating a clear vision and inspiring and motivating others. Not everyone will like what you say, but communication becomes the bridge between confusion and clarity. How do you courageously hold difficult conversations AND keep those people you lead accountable? You must be explicit in what you expect, and be firm on the problems and fair on the person.
- ✓ **Drive Change** – Leadership is about how you deal with change and how you drive change within a team. People don't always like change, but you have to navigate change with resilience and adaptability. Driving change means communication and action. How you communicate, model, and behave will either inspire change or force people to resist based upon your vision, modeling, and response to resistance. It will signal how you help your team adapt, innovate, and grow. In the tense moments of change, find

space to slow down and game plan with these leadership competencies.

✓ **Develop People** — Great leaders develop more leaders. They focus on nurturing talent, empowering others, and creating a culture of continuous learning. Developing people entails believing in people and their potential. You have to get people to believe in their potential, and that may not align with where they are today. Oftentimes, you have to allow the people you are working on developing to not only have their own voice but empower their flair within that voice to be heard. Set a plan to work with people to grow and develop.

✓ **Think Critically** — Leaders have to make tough decisions and accept that not every decision will be liked. This means having the emotional intelligence to understand the current environment and people to make the best decisions for the team. It involves analyzing complex situations, making informed decisions, and solving problems effectively. This helps you navigate challenges and drive strategic outcomes.

✓ **Inspire Others** — True influence comes from authenticity, not authority. When people trust you, respect you, and see you doing the work, they follow readily. They follow your communication, your vision, and your example because you've created a sense of purpose and commitment. Great leaders connect because they know that to lead, you need to engage.

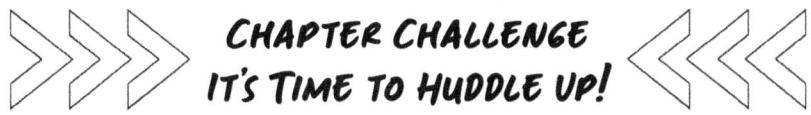

CHAPTER CHALLENGE
IT'S TIME TO HUDDLE UP!

Previously, we talked about the inability to pour from an empty cup. While our cup might be almost empty, we have to deal with the situation regardless of how tired we are. Nonetheless, as ~~Stressed~~ Leaders, scores of people are counting on you. You must utilize short-term stress relievers and leadership competencies, but you also need to create habits that will lead to long-term success.

What can you do to calm mental stress over the long term? Certain habits can promote resilience when facing stress and increase overall wellness. This makes it imperative to create a lifestyle that will ward off stress and deal with challenges in a healthy way, so you can be there to lead everyone else and support their efforts.

My challenge for you: Adopt these long-term habits to allow yourself to lead from the rear at a marathon pace. ~~Stressed~~ Leaders go last when leading others, and you must have built up long-range habits of success to consistently lead from the rear. Habit stack these successful methods for yourself but also for long-range leadership success.

- You are what you eat. Find some form of a diet in which you can be successful. You do not need a seventy-two hour fast once a week, but you must realize that a poor diet can bring greater reactivity to stress. Maybe you are an emotional eater or an unconscious eater, constantly reaching for high-fat, high-sugar foods, which can provide a temporary sense of relief, yet add to your long-term stress. Much like a great morning workout sparks success for the day, a healthy diet of clean eating brings a great amount of brain clarity and productivity. Boxed and processed foods with their refined carbs and chemicals — found in packaged cookies or bagged potato chips — can cause a spike in blood sugar. When your blood sugar crashes, you can experience more stress and anxiety. Clean foods such as vegetables and high protein meats support mood regulation and energy balance. Consuming a healthy diet can help you combat stress over the long haul.
- Find something you love to do that can be a form of leisure. This is a wonderful way to relieve stress. Lifting weights became not only a great workout but something I wanted to do each morning. For others, picking up a hobby like pickleball is a way to relax, compete, and burn calories. Many people feel as though their lives are too busy for hobbies, games, or extra fun. Wallowing away on the couch with streaming services is not the answer as leisure for a healthy lifestyle. Building time

for leisure into your schedule could be key to helping you feel your best. And when you feel better, you'll perform better, which means leisure time may make your work time more efficient.

- Visualize and reinforce success in your head. Keep in mind that it was, and is, always YOU vs. YOU. The way you talk to yourself matters. Self-criticism, self-doubt, and catastrophic predictions aren't helpful. If you're constantly thinking things like, *I don't have time for this* and *I can't stand this* or *I can't do this*, you'll stress yourself out. It's important to learn to talk to yourself in a more realistic, compassionate manner. Instead of calling yourself names or doubting your ability to succeed, utilize a more supportive and successful inner dialogue. We must identify our values, speak life into them, then align our successful behaviors with those habits. Remember: that seed of doubt grows instantly into an uncontrollable weed of self-negativity. Once it starts growing, it is difficult to kill.

- Expressing daily acts of gratitude can be a game changer for your mindset. When you compliment and appreciate others, it elevates your mood. Be grateful for the good things in your life. Scorekeeping or questioning why you don't have more is a self-defeating practice. Gratitude also reminds you of all of the resources you have to cope with stress, which can be empowering. Whether you make it a habit to identify what you're grateful for as you sit around the dinner table, write down things you're grateful for in a daily gratitude journal, or recognize and extend gratitude to others in a face-to-face manner, make gratitude a regular habit. Practicing gratitude can be one of your many habits observed by your children. Live your values in your career and in your practice, but most importantly, take those culture building traits home with you. It is one thing to demonstrate gratitude, or practice integrity at work, but do you show them within the four walls of your home or out in the world for all to see? A simple practice for me is to start and end my days at work and outside of work with joy. Start and end your day with joy by expressing gratitude to someone else. Not only will you see the smile on their face, but your smile will grow too as you leave work and head for home, the most important place to be happy.

- Physical activity is key to managing stress and improving mental health. Join a gym, sign up for a class, or exercise outside. Consistently put competitive dates on your calendar. Keep in mind that there are many different ways to get more physical activity during your day. Implementing a standing desk in your office or taking intentional short walks around the building with daily consistency can change your levels of stress permanently.

- Sometimes, the best way to reduce your stress is to cut something out of your life. Get rid of the things that are adding to your stress so you can experience more peace. For me, instituting temporary phone fasts to reduce distraction and poor time management was a game changer. Maybe it's too much caffeine that has elevated your heart rate and irritability. Making some changes to your daily habits could be instrumental in helping you feel better.

Using these six long-term habits will reduce stress and foster more supportive servant leadership. They can help you prepare for a challenge that will make you uncomfortable and create a growth mindset where you fail forward. Enjoy your wins, knowing that it took failures and losses to achieve those wins. A leader who can successfully navigate stress and have courageous and difficult conversations can thrive. But can you have a meaningful conversation every single day with a stranger? Try it out. Try to find intentional meaning while leaning into a quality conversation with a stranger daily. Approach a parent you don't know yet. Talk to a colleague who most of your team doesn't associate with. Visit with a neighbor you've avoided forever. What you may find is that everyone needs attention, even those who refuse it initially. Eventually, these situations will make you appreciate successful long-range habits that will reduce your stress.

4 ~~stressed~~ LEADERS
DO HARD THINGS

I had been dreading this conversation for a long time. Not because the recipient of the discussion would be upset with me, rather because I was the reason we were having this conversation. It was ENTIRELY on me. I had been challenging myself to "Do Hard Things." It's a mantra I fully embraced, on my terms. Climbing the Manitou Incline multiple times, running my first 10K, then running my first of multiple half marathons – all dates on my calendar, successfully planned, executed, and part of a great journey. However, this hard thing was a conversation I was struggling with. *This Hard Thing,* the hard conversation I needed to have, was with my daughter, Camryn. She was sixteen years old at that moment.

When my daughter was born, I was beyond emotion or words; it was as if I finally realized what my life's purpose was: to be a dad. My daughter has had my heart since the first time I ever laid eyes on her. At that time, I was the head varsity softball coach and assistant football coach at my high school, and my wife had just delivered a beautiful future superstar right into my arms. She wasn't going to be some whiny, soft girl, she was going to be an ass kicker. And I was going to show her the way. Boy, was I naive. We brought her home, and let's just say she was tough. She was an ass kicker, but she was kicking her parents' asses. She was born with a dislocated hip. She needed surgery and would be in a body cast for months. It would require three different sized diapers to change her inside and outside of that cast, for almost nine months. She had colic, and did she ever test our resiliency! So many nights I would lay that frog-legged, casted-up baby girl on my chest to rock her to sleep. Except she wouldn't sleep; she would scream and scream and scream throughout the night. I felt so helpless, but I was determined to get her to sleep.

Then, we found out she had a hemangioma behind her eye. She wore glasses and needed surgery for that too. On her first birthday she had her first febrile seizure. Nothing prepares a parent for a moment of helplessness like your child uncontrollably seizing in front of you. My daughter lay motionless in my arms while my wife hurriedly called 911. Again, I felt helpless panic setting in, not knowing what to do, fearing the worst, expecting the horrible. Watching the volunteer fireman and paramedics in our little village race to revive her... I didn't know what to do. She went on to have more febrile seizures and tested my will each time, continuing to render me helpless and unable to control my response. I still remember playing 1990s grunge rock lullaby CDs while she screamed of colic, rocking her, trying to get her to fall asleep, so I could function at work the next day. I went without sleep most nights for months while working, teaching kids. This happened so many times, but strangely, I miss it.

She played travel softball from the time she was eight until she was a senior in high school, winning many awards. She's strong as an ox and, as a junior, ranked #1 in her high school for strength in the weight room in multiple lifts. At her junior prom, friends, classmates, family – in person and on social media – commented that they could not believe she was the first baseman on the softball team, stunning everyone in her prom dress, wowing the gallery at Prom Walk. I'm sure it was tough having your dad be the Superintendent of your district while in high school, but she didn't complain. She went through her days, her classes, her practices, her games with a great work ethic I am incredibly impressed by.

Yet when she had her first basketball game of the season, she looked slow. How would I tell my hard-working, beautiful daughter that her eating habits were impacting her athleticism? That the same eating habits I struggle with and worry about could impact her for the rest of her life? That she is making the same unconscious decisions I made and, up until recently, never thought about? And what could I do to help her continue to thrive, to continue to kick ass?

It hit me that for seventeen years she watched her father make stupid decisions around food. I struggle as a grazer, an overeater, a snacker, someone who can pound a bag of Cool Ranch Doritos in a sitting. A guy who used to eat twenty wings and a buffalo chicken sandwich and call it lunch. She's seen this along with the hundreds of trips to a gas station before and after practices or games for a donut or cookies. And whether she wants to admit it or not, she is me. We both have the same short fuse, the same killer instinct, the same personality flaws, and she is far too competitive, but she also has some of the same detrimental habits I struggle with, over-eating being one of those.

I have difficult conversations weekly, sometimes daily, in my profession, but admitting to my daughter I had failed her was not a conversation I was looking forward to. I didn't know how to even say it. I didn't want my kid to think I did not value her, that I didn't respect her, that I didn't think she was beautiful, strong, or athletic. SHE IS! She's everything I could ever have hoped to have as a daughter and then some.

How do you tell someone you love they are making bad decisions because they are just like you? You probably thought that Doing Hard Things would be about some complex weight lifting routine, but sometimes a difficult conversation with the people who mean the most to us *IS THE HARD THING*.

I broke down and just went after that tough conversation. I delivered the news to her at a time when I'm sure she wasn't ready: 6:30 AM, before school and work. I needed to get it off my chest that I had failed her and didn't want to see her go through life like I had the last 20+ years – overweight, struggling, lacking confidence in my appearance, constantly questioning my body. She was too darn strong and confident to do that. She may have not even understood the gravity of the conversation, but I needed to have it. She needed to know I didn't want her to have this life I have struggled with. As we sat and talked, it hurt me to admit my failures. It pained me to know she was facing similar self-doubt issues because of the unintended consequences of my poor habits and actions. We choose our hard thing, and I had unintentionally chosen my diet as *the* hard thing; I did not want that for her.

This girl is a champion. She is tenacious, fierce, fabulous, beautiful, and fiery. She should never question herself or lack confidence. But she deserves better for her health, her lifestyle, her betterment, and her future. She doesn't know how hard I had to work out, to watch what I ate, only to lose a pound a week. I don't want her to have to face adversity that is self-inflicted. As we shared our mistakes and self-inflicted pains, I found myself apologizing over and over for creating these unintentional habits in her. It hurt me deeply to admit my failures to the one person who has always counted on me not to fail her. She was not used to seeing Dad apologize, because Dad was tough, Dad led from the front. But, like a true champion, she brushed it off and said, "Dad, I guess we both gotta do better, right?" Fierce, fiery, beautiful, and tenacious – that's my girl!

Humans do not want to seek discomfort, especially discomfort with those we care the most about. We avoid the hard when it comes to a loved one. We choose easy, avoiding discomfort at all costs, for ourselves and sometimes for our children. We have to have the courage to have difficult conversations, to do the hard things that are easier to leave unsaid.

Sometimes, doing hard things is more than a difficult conversation with someone else, maybe it means being honest with yourself. Brutal honesty, such as *how am I handling my relationships?* Not with my spouse or kids, but with my friends. Leadership can be lonely, and the grind of the work and the family time, in many cases, isolates leaders from their friends.

My phone rang. I saw the Caller ID flash on my cell phone to a local number but not a contact. First instinct – telemarketer, second instinct – maybe I should take this, but I don't want to deal with anything work related right now (a frustrated parent, someone from another school). But something deep inside of me said answer the phone, I even tried to doubt it, but the feeling was so strong that I answered. The caller was someone I knew, a friend of a friend, but the message was critical, he said, "Dan, I just talked to Bill…"

My dear friend Bill was a man of loyalty. A man I took for granted, initially. A sportswriter that covered a lot of my team's games, his words were always on point to the temperature of the game, the emotion of the players, and the valor given to the heroes of the moment. I would read his recaps the next day and always smile because Bill was a gifted storyteller and enjoyed covering those games; he loved developing relationships with the players and coaches. He was as genuine a guy as you could find, and it was ALWAYS about writing an article that made the kids and the coaches look great. Bill knew me when my health was at its worst, when the late nights of coaching led to poor health choices. We even shared poor health choices together a few times, with a lot of laughs. When he was named Sportswriter of the Year, I couldn't have been more proud of the man. Our friendship grew, and his adoration for my teams, my daughter, and always asking about my family showed a side of the man I wished everyone would have known.

As a coach, it's natural to be cautious about those from the outside and their intentions. Trust takes years to build, but during tournaments and between games, I often got the chance to connect with Bill on area softball players and teams. Eventually, a friendship formed that went beyond softball. My daughter was very young at this time, maybe five or six years old and was always palling around with the players in the dugout and on the ball diamond. Bill always made time to talk to Cam, to buy her candy or popcorn, and to brag up her dad. It's easy to think it was just a nice guy making a nice gesture, but as the years went on, I realized it was genuine. Cam got older, started swinging the bat herself, and Bill would ask about her games and how she was doing. Humbly, I would not embellish her abilities, but as she aged, her game got better and better. I would share that success with Bill, and he would smile that big smile and belly laugh at my continued humble disbelief.

One cold spring day, during the end of my high school coaching career, while I was also coaching Cam's travel team, Bill told me he was going to make a game. His health was fading, and he had told me several times before that he would make the trek to a far away tournament. But life has a funny way of complicating things. My schedule and my job demands put many relationships and special moments on the back burner. There was always SOMETHING going on, SOMETHING pulling me towards my job. And Bill was the same, always covering a game somewhere in and out of our area. When the local small town newspaper was bought out by a larger corporation, within minutes, jobs were eliminated, and even Bill was forced into covering different areas. Sadly, in my final year of coaching, he was covering our team less and less. Our phone tag became more and more common, with a text here and there, an unopened voicemail becoming the norm.

If I'm being perfectly transparent and honest, sometimes when that caller ID popped up, it meant that it was going to be a LONG phone call, and I'd let it go to voicemail. I was too busy. I didn't have time to take the call right then because I was too busy with my job. I WAS TOO BUSY TO BE THE FRIEND HE DESERVED.

As we both got older, Bill wasn't able to make many of Cam's games, but one day he said he was coming to watch her play when she was 13. That tournament was near his house, but it was an awful Illinois spring weather event. Cold, rainy, windy, nasty, nowhere anybody wanted to be playing softball. I texted Bill, thinking about his fading health and said something to the effect of "Yep, tourney on, unreal, stay home, it's brutal out." He responded almost immediately, "I'll be there."

And there he was, the same Bill, sporting that same blue sweatshirt he loved to wear, cheering our team on from the first row of the bleachers, proudly boasting about how special this group would be at the high school, how much of a moron I was to be walking away from it to chase the dream of becoming a superintendent. Bill enjoyed mocking me for finally building a state championship contending program, only to hand the keys over to someone else. On this awful and miserable day, Bill was the warmest guy there, cheering, laughing, yelling, and just being Bill, the fan.

It was late in the tournament, in the championship game, and we were playing a much larger suburban team who brought in players from all over the state. Like cinematic magic, Cam came up in a critical situation: late in the game, down a run, two on base, worked a tough count against a fireball-throwing pitcher, fouling off pitch after pitch, until BOOM! Like a fairy tale, she drove a ball into right center for a three run bomb. It was her first ever home run in a travel softball tournament. I vividly remember everything about that moment because I was so proud, not just for the home run but for the years of work this kid had put in to finally see that success pay off. I remember seeing Bill in his bright blue sweatshirt jumping up and down, clapping, loudly hootin' and hollerin' for my kid. As she headed back to the dugout. Bill bee-lined directly for that dugout to talk to her, like he was interviewing the game MVP for one of his great stories.

As I stepped away from coaching the varsity team and headed down the administrative path in our district, Bill and I tried to regularly stay in touch. But due to the complications of the corporate newspaper takeover, COVID, and my lack of coaching, we weren't as close as we used to be.

A few years later, I was in Las Vegas walking on the Strip, and my phone buzzed; it was Bill. I took the call, and he told me he was going in for exploratory surgery. I couldn't believe it. There I was, in a warm paradise, while this guy was going through hell, lying in a hospital bed, unsure of what was to come. It hit hard. I felt I hadn't been the friend he deserved or been there for him like I should have been. I was missing perspective, and he deserved better loyalty from me.

I checked in regularly with Bill after that, and the news continued to get worse and worse, until he was admitted to the ICU. He was placed into a medically induced coma, and I was getting updates from a family friend. Days went by, and it didn't look good. I thought for sure, at any moment I would get the call and have to explain to my daughter, one of his biggest fans, that we had a funeral to attend.

Unfortunately, Bill's condition worsened. Our talks grew more difficult; I tried to make him laugh, but he was not in a great place. Then, one day when I checked in, miraculously, he was back to the old Bill, even watching his future daughter-in-law play basketball online at the collegiate level. He was diagramming plays for me, laughing about old stories involving coaching rivalries I had, he was back! I got to tell him how much I loved him and how much he meant to me. That talk put so many things in my life in perspective, the job stress I worry about, the development of my children, the wife of mine who doesn't get near enough attention, the way I try to be present for so many things in my life and fail so miserably because my plate is too full. This new enlightenment was something I needed: being thankful for one more conversation each day, being present for just one more moment. I wish the story had a happier ending, but it does not. Within a couple of days of that final conversation where he seemed to be improving, he was gone.

I should have done more to be a better friend to Bill, especially during the years when COVID crippled his writing career, where his health deteriorated so fast, but I was too busy to take a phone call. It's embarrassing to admit the reality; I wasn't there for my friend in the last couple of years of our friendship when he needed me the most. To this day, I still kick myself for not being a more present friend for Bill.

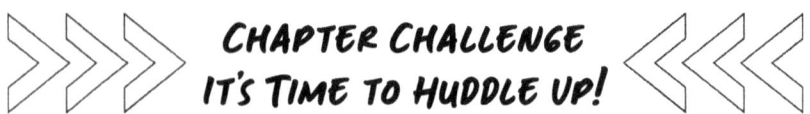

Doing Hard Things means something different to everyone. You probably didn't anticipate the hard things in this chapter being a difficult conversation with a loved one or an honest self-reflection. Rather, you probably expected me to pontificate about strength training badassery. I've developed a mental cookie jar of badass cookies that I stockpile when I do something that is, well, badass. Each time I knock a date off a calendar or hit a new personal record in weightlifting, I throw a cookie in that mental jar. On mile nine of my first half marathon, when my right leg was barking at me, my hip was aching, and my groin was tight, there was no chance in hell I was going to walk. I had deposited way too many badass cookies in my mental cookie jar to quit or to allow myself to give up due to a little pain. I continue to put dates on the calendar, constantly challenging myself to Do Hard Things.

I had lost one hundred pounds, but I was in a rut, stuck because I was half-in and half-out of a diet and workout plan. I wasn't fully committed. One evening, I had been mindlessly scrolling X when a post from a guy I had seen a couple times appeared again. I decided to follow him and over the next month or so as his posts kept speaking to me, resonating with what I was going through. After enough posts, I decided to sign up for an event he was keynoting in Colorado. This was my Do Hard Things challenge – stepping out of my comfort zone, tackling something completely out of my norm even if I doubted it at first.

In August of 2023, I picked up my rental car at the Colorado Springs airport, and embarked on my first Do Hard Things event, the Manitou Incline. That 2,900 step mountain did its best to conquer me. At about step 2,000 I was mentally ready to quit, but I told myself if I was going to Do Hard Things, this was the first brick to stack. This was foundational and not a loss I was willing to take. Eventually, I conquered the beast in 57 minutes, hitting my goal time!

Standing at the apex of the climb, I was jubilant. I'm sure the smile on my face was ear-to-ear when I was done! At the summit I was met with high fives, smiles, and congratulatory remarks from fellow achievers. Now, I had to get down that mountain on the Bear Trail and back to my sister's house to check in to the conference – without time to rest. The three-mile hike down was a bit of a time crunch, but I had to get to the conference.

I had done cold plunges with hydrotherapy in Mexico multiple times, so I wasn't nervous. But their idea of a cold plunge was mid 50s water temperature in 90-degree heat. Fresh ice in 33 degrees would be a bit different I assumed. I was here to stack bricks, to consistently win each event in the challenge of YOU vs. YOU.

I volunteered to go first amongst more than one hundred people I did not know. This community was one that surprised me, lots of jacked, tanned dudes chanting, "Let's go!" when the 265 pound heavy man volunteered to go first. A guy named Jay led me through some helpful breathing exercises, then I was ready. An enthusiastic "Best Day Ever!" from one of the guys, and future coach, met me as I entered the ice bath. My legs immediately tingled like I was seeing an acupuncturist.

As I slowly submerged myself, I knew this was the beginning of a journey; I was at the beginning of a metamorphosis. A minute or so into the ice bath, I said *Screw it* and submerged myself fully under the water for a few seconds. For the first time in a LONG while, I felt alive. I felt like I did when I would straddle the rubber on the pitcher's mound in high school, in control, ball in my hand, ready to dominate someone.

A year later, I went back to Colorado Springs, knocked eight full minutes off my Manitou Incline and set the tone for the ice bath. With one year in the books of focused, dedicated efforts to Doing Hard Things, my ~~Stressed~~ Leader's Journey had not only shocked my system, but people at the conference were inspired by my confidence and overall transformation.

The effects of the ice bath saved my weary legs, but I could also feel my body opening up, not tensing up – releasing toxins and stress. While the ice bath shocked my system, it also set off a chain of reactions that have catapulted my life from a stressed-out, rage-filled leader to a calm and focused man who lifts heavy weights, runs long distances, and focuses each day on living his Best Day Ever by challenging myself to continually Do Hard Things. Since that conference, I have been back multiple times to that incline, which serves as a metaphor for my life. I have improved my time every single time I climb those 2,900 steps, focused my breathing on each ice-bath, and emerged stronger each day of my journey.

My challenge for you: What is your hard thing? Is it putting a date on the calendar and executing a game plan with incentives along the way? Can you keep adding badass cookies to your cookie jar? Can you remove the governor from your brain, like I did – in pain – during that half marathon? There is nothing special about me, just a guy who wakes up each morning and says Day One, Let's Go! If you want real resilience, you have to put yourself in uncomfortable situations, into hard things. Those hard things may even knock you down a peg. When I went to bench 300 pounds for the first time, my coach pointed out everything wrong in my form. I was dejected. I was so close, but he told me to lower the weight and improve my technique, control, focus, and breathing before attempting to hit that landmark number. How do we fight immediate gratification, comfort, and justifications that lead to softness, victimhood, and unhappiness? We do that by continually Doing Hard Things. We are callusing our mind to train those weak qualities out of existence. You've worked hard by challenging yourself to Do Hard Things, to set dates on the calendar, to build habits of success, but you've messed up along the way too. Don't be a victim to those losses; you have earned them, and they've callused your mind, built up your resilience. There is tremendous wisdom gained in any loss, from every failure. Do not define yourself by the times you fell, even if it was for 20 years. Define yourself by the times you get up and finish. I refuse to take a zero every day because of stress management habits. I won't let the marathon with achy legs and mental manipulations slow down my progress. I simply won't quit.

Failure is where your resilience builds, more and more with every loss, each stumbling point, another scraped knee, damaged ego, more bumps and bruises, when you decide to get back up... **one more time.**

Anyone who played high school football knows the joy, excitement, and pain of Friday Night Lights. We remember the bonds of brotherhood, the brutal two-a-days, the emotional defeats, the embarrassing and, sometimes, glorifying film sessions. But as we age, those days become distant memories. As life happens, competition morphs into fun and more relaxing times: boating and camping, attending events to watch other athletes compete. Looking back, you realize the competition itch has started to fade. Being a spouse and parent suddenly fills most of your time, and you spend it on the couch watching *Phineas and Ferb* with your kids, snacking on some Cool Ranch Doritos, not sure how it all happened… it just did.

In adulthood, I didn't have my Center screaming, "Huddle up!" after the chaos of the last play so I could refocus on my next blocking assignment. I had my wife and kids to be accountable to, but my wife wasn't shouting at me to be accountable to my left tackle on this next trap play. I didn't have my Center to get my mindset right and not let him down. Little did I realize I was letting my family down by not being accountable for my own health. I needed to Huddle Up in life. I needed to get back in the game and refocus on the next play.

As my weight gain continued, it took me years to figure out I needed that competitive edge back. I needed those competition dates on the calendar. What I didn't realize is I needed other men to help me understand what I was missing. I needed a community. I was searching for that spark, that push, that accountability piece to get me over the hump.

Surrounding myself with a group of like-minded individuals in an online, hybrid-workout community was exactly the spark I didn't realize I was craving. I loved reading their stories, listening to them on Zoom calls, hearing about their 100K racing competitions, their backyard ultra races, their ironman competitions, their strength goals, their powerlifting meets, and I found myself wanting. Not wanting to catch their success but wanting to have the same vibe, the same optimism, the same energy, the same push to refuse to fail.

Huddling up with this crew, all of whom I knew only as an online community group, was paramount for me. The 4:30 AM alarm would go off, and I didn't want to let twelve guys down. The initial surge of the community faded off in time for some people, but I refused to allow that to happen to me. Maybe they were grinding in silence and just didn't vocalize as much as me, but that sharing of wisdom and tagging along on another's journey kept providing the push I needed. I was active in the group chats, and it became the sense of community I needed to push myself and feel accountable to these other guys. My efforts within the group were not about pushing the other guys, it was about pushing myself. It was the eternal war of ME vs. ME, my brain wanting to sleep in, my body saying *Take the day off,* where comfort wars with discipline.

After 12 weeks, the community group ended. I still had a half marathon to run coming up, my longest run ever. The last five miles of that 13-mile run were a constant mental war of ME vs. ME. I told myself before that race, I would not walk a single step. During that trying mental time, I thought about a lot of tricks my coach had taught me.

- Think of how proud your wife and kids will be of you.
- Think of how much work you've put in to get to this point.
- Think of what you ask yourself daily, "Am I paying the price today to achieve the greatness I want in life?" Pay the price in this run right now!
- The other guys in the group were running 50K's, 100K's, full marathons, ironman's, I can certainly do a half marathon and refuse to walk a step.
- When it came to the several hills, especially late in the race, I screamed in my brain what my coach told me to, "FU** them hills!" and I sprinted up them – well, it felt like a sprint, but probably wasn't much of one. Nevertheless, it worked!

I finished the race without walking, my legs were heavy, my knees were barking, but I couldn't help smiling. None of this would have happened, without the support of that community. Who knew a 12-week commitment of being all in, not skipping days, not skipping reps, would get me there. Throughout those 12 weeks, I dropped about 15 more pounds, and the inches flew off my body in critical areas.

Consistency, focus, and discipline will take you further in a few months than hope and dreams. Where comfort meets discipline is a crossroads in our journey as a ~~Stressed~~ Leader. When you don't lean into those relationships that have the potential to keep you accountable, humble, and striving, you further isolate yourself as a Stressed Leader. It is paramount that we NOT isolate ourselves but lean in and lean on our community for support.

Sometimes our community lies in our workplace, but other times our network outside of our usual inner circle begs for help. That day started out like any other Friday in the grays of Illinois: a cold blustery winter day. It was Funnel Cake Friday, part of our RISE program encouraging positive student actions through three simple tenets: *Be Here, Be Kind, and Be Accountable*. A simple reward for displaying strong character. I started the day at 4:45 AM with my workout, then headed home to shower and wake the kiddo's up for school. I got to school and started my day with joy, as always. I had prepared for my weekly Administrative Cabinet meeting and wanted to go over the agenda before our planned meeting that morning. The coffee was flowing as I extended gratitude to my rockstar Chief School Business Official. Truly, the morning was going well. The cabinet meeting was filled with great discussions amongst a great cabinet of leaders. After the meeting I had scheduled a reflective phone call with another superintendent about the upcoming ~~Stressed~~ Leaders Retreat I was planning. Here is where the day began to spiral in a manner I did NOT expect...

This phone call was the EXACT reminder I needed from my community and the EXACT purpose of why I was doing this, why I was planning this retreat and coaching community. A young fellow superintendent was sharing some of the unfortunate situations he was dealing with in his career at that time. Like me, we had both been tested, pushed, measured, and manipulated by folks with agendas. We had been in the trenches, and at times, it had gotten ugly. As he shared his story of personal attacks, threats to him and his family, and lies spread about his family, I felt for this guy. While I'd had some frustrating people to deal with in the public sector, what he expressed made me hurt for him. I reminded him, "It's just a job. Remember what is important. Remember who is waiting for you each night behind that front door. Someone else will always sit in this desk chair after us. Don't let them get to you; the loudest boos always come from the cheap seats." We had a great discussion, and we focused on the one aspect of the job that can be the most difficult – ISOLATION.

The job of a leader is lonely and can be incredibly isolating. You don't get into a leadership position for the attaboy, for glad handing, or for acknowledgement. You do the job because you have passion, charisma, and are relentless in your pursuit to make something better than it was before you arrived. It can be quite lonely, especially when you are under attack and do not have a network to interact with, to vent to, to bounce ideas and solutions off of. There aren't many leaders in your buildings, especially the higher you get, who understand your plight, who can appreciate the anxiety, who can maneuver the tense moments with strict faith, determination, poise, and hopefully, a smile.

There's a certain toughness and lack of vulnerability that most leaders have. Most leaders are unable to show vulnerability as they perceive it as a weakness, a gap, a blindside that could be exploited. We do not want to appear weak. We want people to trust us, to know that we have all of the answers – "Ask Dan, he will know how to handle this." As I listened to this man, who I greatly value, admire, and respect, I apologized that he had to deal with this tough situation. I reminded him that his family is everything; that the job is just that, a job. But I also reminded him that I would always be there for him if he needed anything. Just make the call; send the text. The entirety of this conversation was gripping my heart, appreciating the pain of my friend.

As I resumed my day, completing my Board of Education weekly memo, visiting students at lunch to see the Friday Funnel Cakes, joking with our secretaries about the Dean of Students, I couldn't get the idea of my friend receiving death threats from a community member over school leadership out of my mind. I stopped in my tracks and sent him a text. It was simple, "We got this buddy. We're here for each other in good times and bad." He responded right away, "You don't know how much I needed that talk today. Thank you." Such a simple reinforcement, a reminder why we Huddle Up: leaders need community. We cannot do this alone and should not try. Damn our pride! Towards the end of the day, I still had this man's problems on my mind. I had so many questions, so many ideas to help him, but I also didn't want to overwhelm him. In leadership positions, we can become a prisoner of the moment, captivated by what sits right in front of us, tunnel vision focusing on only this item – when there are other priorities that need to be addressed.

As the day wound down, I got another message from a different leader. The third leader in a week, calling me, telling me that he was struggling. I shook my head in frustration and texted him, "I'm here, Chief. Make the call." He called, and we spoke for what seemed like an hour about the numerous problems he was facing. It is his first year as building principal, and the guy is working his tail off but running into brick walls at every turn. From staff unwilling to grow, parents questioning his discipline methods, coaches who are members of the RDA club (Rules Don't Apply to me), and a board member cutting his knees out, he was struggling. He said to me, "Maybe I need to just go back to the classroom. I'm not sure I'm cut out for this." *C'mon man! Not cut out for this? You are a legend; you've been through the wars. You were a head coach, department chair, instructional leader, and now you're a building principal. You are one of the strongest men I know,* I thought to myself. I gave him a good motivational talk about the first year in a major leadership position being the toughest, the concept of failing and failing to learn, the grays of a midwest winter running up to Christmas break, etc. He needed some time away from the job. I told him to go home, fast from his cell phone (the emails will be there Saturday morning), lean into some time with his kids and wife, and even if it's just going to dinner or grabbing a pizza for home, tune in to the conversations and be present. Remember what you've done, what is important, your North Star.

I went through my workout, blasted some rock music in my headphones throughout the grind but could not get these two men out of my head. Both of these men – my friends, my colleagues, young leaders – were trying to do these jobs to their fullest potential and then some, but both were drowning. Their problems were different, but they were the same: someone challenging them, coming at them from many angles, and feeling consumed by the pressures of it all but handling it by themselves, in isolation. Isolating yourself is not the answer. We need each other and have to be there to support each other to keep us all in the game, thriving.

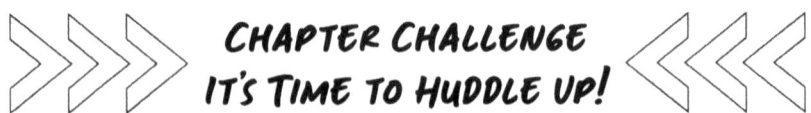

Chapter Challenge: It's Time to Huddle Up!

You have shocked your system by getting up off the mat. You've chosen to lead yourself first, while also serving others. You've committed to doing hard things, no matter if that is a difficult conversation or putting a date on the calendar with a competition.

My challenge for you: Join a community of like-minded leaders. Chances are, even though the variables differ, we are going through the same problems, and they are the things that keep us up at night.

The ~~Stressed~~ Leaders Community exists to keep our leaders together; Huddle Up with the close network of a team to help build relationships. Our online community is one of true leaders who are currently in the mess. Not theory, not professional development exercises that work in a vacuum but real leaders with real problems looking for real solutions one day at a time, one text at a time, one Zoom call at a time. Our online community has not only leadership resources with practical solutions to tough situations but offers weekly Zoom opportunities for leadership coaching, sharing of information, and bouncing ideas off of each other. My ~~Stressed~~ Leaders Community, available on the Telegram Messaging app, offers accountability, collaboration with people in similar stations in life, fighting for the same successes and going through the same obstacles you face with resources at your disposal.

Even if it's not the ~~Stressed~~ Leaders Community, find one that works for you. Don't work and live in isolation. As ~~Stressed~~ Leaders we must Huddle Up with other district or building leaders to discuss these concepts. As a leader, it is far too easy to avoid vulnerability and communication, especially when you are unsure or lack confidence. Being vulnerable is the opposite of a weakness; it takes courage to have more of these difficult conversations. Growth requires courage, and courage can grow within a team.

Conclusion

~~stressed~~
LEADERS
NEED PERSPECTIVE

In chapter 4, I told you a story about my dear friend Bill. At his funeral, seeing all of the pictures of Bill with his kids made me appreciate the man and friend of mine. Anytime you walk through a wake or a funeral line you have to step back and contemplate your own lifetime. My only thought was about my wife and kids. I found myself regretting my lack of commitment to my friends but justifying such because of my family and my career. The career I had dreamt of and loved was also a time thief to my relationships.

When your job is also your passion and it consumes you, it never stops. It's a part of the job that I love, the constant fight or flight reaction to the two-minute drill, the intensity, the pressure, the calling. When a crisis hits, everyone's eyes and attention turn to you. Some people, like myself, are addicted to that type of energy. But with such an addiction comes a loss of perspective and a loss of appreciation of the real things that matter in life. When your job consumes you, you lose the ability to make space, create margins, remove items from your full plate, or find time to think and appreciate what matters most.

I'm constantly reminding myself to make space, to find time to step back, think, reflect, and not simply react. My wife is great at reminding me that I am often distant and not present in the moment because there is some "crucial" thought going through my head. Even as I was driving to my great friend Bill's funeral with my wife, I was contemplating a long-range plan about the science labs and partnerships for our student's career goals. WHERE WAS MY PERSPECTIVE!? The job controlled my brain at times, and at a time when I should have been focused on where I was about to go and what I was about to see, I was thinking about my job?

Gathering perspective often happens in the aftermath of a life-defining moment. I should have been focused on the now and the impact of that moment, not the distraction of work. Unfortunately, the gravity of decisions you make at work sometimes occupy more of your brain than the decisions you are making now with your family. Regardless of your time on or off at work or home, the impacts of our decision-making as a ~~Stressed~~ Leader are monumental.

- Did I make the wrong decision?
- Did that decision and its consequences send me down a wrong path?
- Did that path leave a wound I am trying to heal?
- Did I overreact in that situation and hurt someone?
- Was the someone I hurt a person who means everything to me?
- Did my lack of perspective leave me not appreciating those relationships that matter the most?
- Was I not there for someone I needed to be because I was occupied by my career?

Finding perspective is a humbling reality. We all know it, but can you admit it is the truth? Honest self-reflection about your pace and how you spend your time on and off is a critical step on the way to finding perspective. We must remember that as leaders, we set the pace. So, what about your current pace? In chapter one I explained to you that I would schedule vacations and on each trip, I would find myself in a less than favorable state because I had *earned it*. Time off won't heal you when the problem is in how you spend your time *ON*. How do you spend your time on? In my position, I am ALWAYS on. I can reflect honestly and say I was (and am) always on, even if it was strolling into the local hardware store on a Saturday. Before I began to break away from being a Stressed Leader, I was ready and willing to talk shop with anyone at any time. I was checking emails at night and responding to them. I needed to find space. Being leaders, we know that work is a primary source of stress in our lives, and having a leadership role increases the level of such stress. We also know we are so successful on paper or in appearance because we feel the need to always be on. We see it often in executive, district, or building leadership: working at a frenetic and unsustainable pace, just trying to make it to the next break. We finally make it to the break and think we are refreshed, only to feel like there was no break at all as we fall back into our familiar habits. A sustainable pace is the cure for an unsustainable pace, not taking quick mini vacations.

As I think about being a leader at work and striving to model the hero at home, being where my feet are is a current focus. Instead of appreciating the current success or happiness, I used to focus too much on the future vacations. I would finally have some quality time off; yet, the extended break would not change anything unless I changed how I spent my current time on. I knew my unsustainable pace needed to change for me, my family, and the entire staff.

Most leaders do not want to hear or talk about work-life balance or self-care. They want to get the job done on their terms, and many are unwilling to be vulnerable. In previous chapters, we shared strategies to cope with short-term, long-term, and even self-inflicted stress. The temporary removal from stressful situations through self-care tactics is essential, but it will not have a significant, long-term impact on the health and longevity of leaders. It is time for Stressed Leaders to honestly and genuinely reflect on how they spend their time on through the day to day and week to week. Self-care not only involves much-needed time off, but revamping what time on looks like. Many building or district leaders are working at an unsustainable pace that has and will ultimately have a detrimental impact on themselves, their families, their students, staff, and schools.

The process of obtaining a sustainable pace begins with honest self-reflection. During the unsustainable pace, Stressed Leaders are often unable to stop *doing* long enough to *think*. That two-minute drill clock is counting down, and it is easy to spring into action, desperately wanting to put out the fires and their backdraft. But you must slow down and not only find your pace but control your pace. By controlling your pace, you will have a greater capacity to work with the staff to control their pace. But how can YOU control your pace within that two-minute drill?

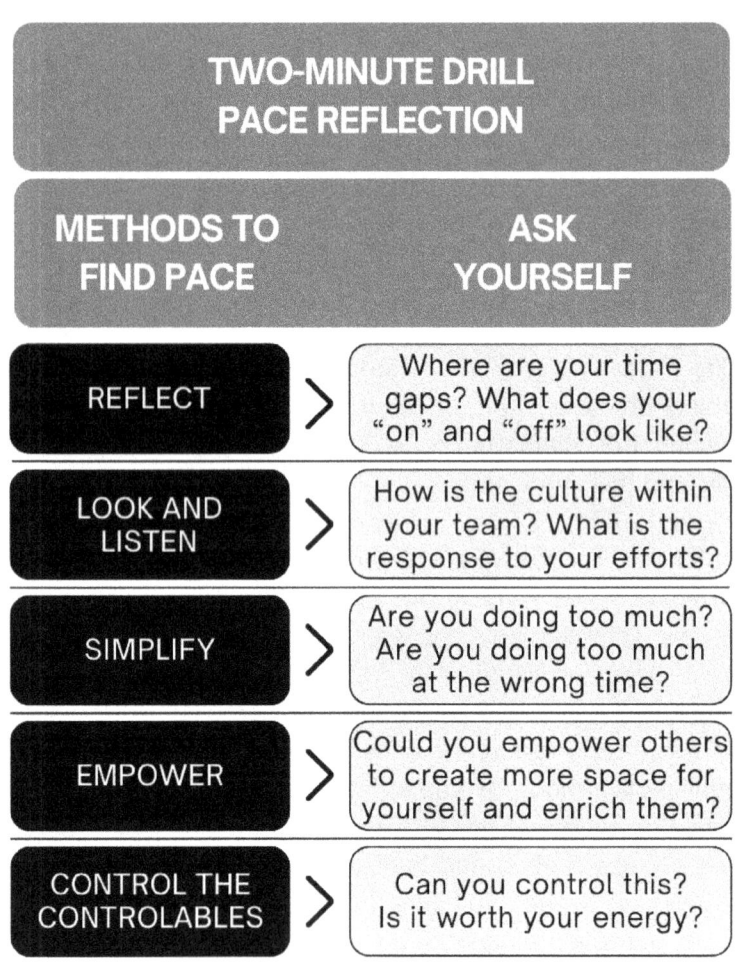

1. **Reflect**
    - How are you spending your time on?
    - Spend some time documenting your day-to-day and week-to-week schedule.
        - When are you most productive or least productive?
        - Where are your time gaps or time wasters?
        - Do your days align with your vision and mission, or have they become a never-ending to-do list with no clear focus?
    - How do you feel physically, mentally, and emotionally?

2. **Look and Listen**
   - What are teachers and staff saying?
     - How are they feeling?
   - What is your family saying?
     - How are they feeling?
   - What trends do you notice:
   - When a crisis arises and you enter the two-minute drill to put out fires, what does it look like after the fire has been extinguished?
     - Are the embers still smoldering?
   - What is the current culture of the building?
   - How about the culture at home?
     - As those close to you to provide you with honest feedback without judgment.
3. **Simplify**
   - Are you trying to do too much?
   - Are you trying to do too much at the wrong times?
   - What are your district or building priorities?
     - How can you simplify those priorities to a few focused areas?
   - What can be removed from your plate to create more efficiency, more space and better results?
4. **Empower**
   - Are there areas you can empower others through delegation?
   - Can you put others in their strength zones to allow you and those who follow to work at your and their absolute best?
5. **Control the Controllables**
   - What areas are you trying to control that are not within your control?
   - Have you found these areas draining your mental and physical energy?

- Are you wasting time focusing on problems that aren't really your concern, that may even distract you from your focus?

As building leaders, it is time to set the example of self-care through not only how we spend our time off, but how we spend our time on. It is essential to take time to reflect on what we are asking of ourselves and others. First and foremost, we are in the business of people, and we need to take care of ourselves to best take care of all those around us. If we don't, we will continue to fall into a vicious cycle of exhausting ourselves towards a break, spending the time off trying to recover only to exhaust ourselves once again.

"I'm too blessed in my career to be stressed," I often joke to others. In truth, it's a terrible joke. There is an absence of perspective that comes with leadership. A good friend of mine, Dan Cox, used to begin his keynote speeches with, "My name is Dan Cox, I'm a husband, a father, a brother, a Christian, a teacher, and a Superintendent, but being a Superintendent is not who I am." Dan will admit to you today that he, like many Superintendents, allowed the job to consume him and be his entire identity. While he might say he was not only a Superintendent, that wasn't true. The job defined him until the job was taken away from him in the span of one decision. He will tell you that perspective is a humbling reality. We are all stressed, no matter the amount of tools and tricks we use to combat stress. If we don't make long-term, sustainable habit changes in our loops, this career will consume us. The challenge becomes: are you ready to break away from being a Stressed Leader, and take the actions to change your habits to transform into the ~~Stressed~~ Leader you were always capable of becoming to everyone in your life?

AFTERWORD

~~stressed~~
LEADERS
RETREAT

"There's not enough time in the day to lead the district in the manner that I want to lead our students and staff. I AM DROWNING!"

A colleague of mine said this to me at the end of another school year, and it caused me great heartache. This is a great man, someone I would follow, a great leader, and an even better person. To hear him admit he was drowning and contemplating leaving the profession was beyond troubling. I felt something pulling at me to help him, but I didn't have the words in the moment to help him out. I tried to support him, told him all of the great things he was doing in his district, mentioned the success of their baseball team that spring, and he nodded his head along, but the look in his eyes told a completely different story. I felt the gut punch when he responded with, "So..." He was beaten, he was defeated. I checked in on him regularly and wasn't surprised when he told me he was leaving the profession and accepting a job in the business sector. A man with over twenty years of experience in education was pulling the plug because he was burned out. The onslaught of parental demands, the toxic staff members, the apathetic students had all beaten him. I implored him to reconsider. I told him these things were the minorities in all of this, but his mind was made up; he was done. He told me,

"I'm tired. I'm tired of losing each day."

The journey of a leader is one of ups and downs, some losses, and some great wins. We've all had moments of struggle and strife, but we've also all had moments of awe and built relationships that have been pivotal in our lives. When that exit phone call came that day in June, I realized I had a calling; there was a greater purpose for my educational journey. I needed to become a coach for educational leaders and help my fellow leaders through the trials and tribulations to build a tribe of like-minded leaders through a community of ~~Stressed~~ Leaders who rise above those forces trying to pull us down.

I have developed a one of a kind leadership retreat, based on preventing burn out and getting Stressed Leaders back in the game. Typically, as educational leaders, we attend leadership conferences where we sit in a hotel ballroom, listen to an inspirational author present their message in front of a couple hundred educators, we applaud, and then go about our routine or maybe spend some time networking. We might attend break out sessions where we sit around and listen to an expert, we applaud, and we head to the lobby bar. We spend thousands of dollars to attend these seminars, where maybe we grab a nugget or two of good information to bring back to our school, implement for a short while, then rinse and repeat each year.

This conference system may work for some people, but the way we try to lead our staff and students has changed, and the accountability on our leadership shoulders has increased. The demands are growing, and the results have diminished. We need something **DIFFERENT**. We need action and purpose. We don't earn action and purpose with "sit and get" seminars and drinks with our buddies at the lobby bar. Don't misunderstand, sharing drinks and laughs with our network is important, but is that why we attend these conferences? Does it solve the problem of our stress levels?

Today, we have more people judging and berating our leadership on social media. From firing the basketball coach to showing up at the board meeting with pitchforks, it feels like we are constantly under attack. People are telling our story without an ounce of concern for the people who know the real story: the Stressed Leader who fights daily to tell the real story, who shows up day in and day out, in the trenches with the teachers, trying to lead the district. There are three groups that constantly challenge our purpose and intentions, distracting us from what matters:

- The aggressive parents who have their sights set on the bullseye on your back.
- The toxic staff member who whispers in corners critiquing your leadership.

- The student who simply doesn't care and doesn't want to be at school.

Those three groups occupy much of our time. Not only do they live in our head rent-free, they've welcomed the squatters in who want to pile on. It's easy to see how leaders can struggle when this is the focus of your mind. So, why this retreat, and how is it going to get educational leaders back into the game?

The ~~Stressed~~ Leaders Retreat exists to help passionate people avoid burnout & stay in the game. We accomplish this by providing unique, rejuvenating experiences that connect leaders to a tribe of other like-minded leaders for long-term coaching and support.

THE FIRST ~~STRESSED~~ LEADERS RETREAT EVENT
First, ~~Stressed~~ Leaders need to SHOCK THE SYSTEM! As I plunged deep into my first ice bath in the mountains of Colorado, I felt awakened. Retreat attendees heard my story, my message of how I went from an excuse making *I'll start tomorrow* to a *Seize-the-day*. I shared with the group how I found gratitude in those growing pains. I delivered a message of pain that many leaders often suffer from, sacrificing time and energy with loved ones because of their career, because of the need to be the best, to strive for success.

As we shared introductions, some attendees were skeptical; they were concerned about some of the same fears I had: imposter syndrome, fear of failure, and a fear of being vulnerable in front of other leaders. Knowing the first activity after my keynote was an ice bath had some leaders truly questioning their attendance. From the jump off point, Joe – a veteran high school principal – was questioning why he was doing this. He was *not* going to take that ice plunge. Yet as the momentum built and leader after leader took the plunge, Joe reluctantly stepped to the plate. He took the plunge, with a smile even, and while he was doubtful, he grew throughout the event, even remarking, "I was a bit skeptical at first, especially with the ice plunge, but the retreat was more than I ever expected. Taking care of me was really put into perspective. I have been making what would be considered a small commitment to working out, being healthier, attempting to lower my blood pressure, etc. The ideas I gathered from the retreat have lit a fire to push me to commit to doing more hard things and shocking my system." Opening one's mind and body to a new experience can be revolutionary.

Next, ~~Stressed~~ Leaders need to GO FIRST. What's your purpose? How are you making your mark? How are you leading your school, your family? Mike Donatelli, the leader of the Best Day Ever Community, took the stage on that sunny day outside, leading from the front, addressing a deck full of leaders, empowering them to finally put themselves first. As Stressed Leaders, we are not fulfilling our potential as adults, as spouses, as parents, as educators, or as leaders. A ~~Stressed~~ Leader should put dates on the calendar, then cross the line triumphantly!

~~Stressed~~ Leaders SERVE OTHERS. Our third keynote speaker had a message of inspiration but also of heartache from getting divorced with young children to managing her life with cancer. Her message was to serve our people fully and to find and harness moments of gratitude during adversity.

Her keynote was gripping and powerful as we experienced a sunset cruise of the Illinois River. Wine and water was an experience that all ~~Stressed~~ Leaders enjoyed aboard the St. Genevieve, navigating the riverway through Buffalo and Starved Rock canyons.

On our second day of the retreat, attendees were met back at the camp with coffee and snacks to start the day. But before that was an Earn Your Sunrise endurance run that started our day with a spark. Running through the quiet Illinois River Valley and Fox River waterway trails at sunrise was a great start to day two. Next on day two, we experienced a keynote from a professional entrepreneur photographer whose message resonated with leaders who, at times, do not elevate their own image. Think of presidential photos or CEO headshots. As leaders we don't often put ourselves in that portrait. Remember, our self-talk tells our story. His keynote came with a professional portrait and multiple tools to help the ~~Stressed~~ Leader elevate themself on this journey.

As the morning continued, the fifth keynote highlighted that ~~Stressed~~ Leaders Need to DO HARD THINGS. The speaker's message was captivating, presenting to our attendees how he Does Hard Things as a runner, a rucker, and an endurance athlete. While also being a father, a superintendent, and a ~~Stressed~~ Leader, he led the group through his life journey and inspired all of the attendees to Do Hard Things with a focus on willpower.

After the conclusion of his keynote, we took the short trek to Starved Rock State Park where he brought with him an arsenal of ruck vests, weights, and assorted other goodies. The group was challenged to grow together to carry every one of these heavy things throughout Starved Rock State Park, *together*. A two-mile ruck through some of the most breathtaking views of the Illinois River Valley area was completed by all of our leaders, and as we downed water in the lodge parking lot, we could feel the sense of accomplishment radiating throughout the group.

After building up a tremendous appetite, our final keynote explained how ~~Stressed~~ Leaders Need HUDDLE UP. Being a part of a community is essential for those who feel like they are drowning – to have someone to lean on and hold them accountable and push them to new heights. The ~~Stressed~~ Leaders Community will do just that for our leaders everywhere. From fitness and workout advice, to a social media platform to share wisdom and concerns, this community offers our leaders a great opportunity to support each other. The ~~Stressed~~ Leaders Community is more than an app, more than a social media messaging platform; it is personal and professional accountability and respect, a place for all of us to lean on each other and lean into the lifestyle, the movement, that is ~~STRESSED~~ LEADERS. The ~~Stressed~~ Leaders Retreat was the first of its kind, a game changer for the leadership community.

ABOUT THE AUTHOR

Dan Stecken is an educator with over twenty-one years of leadership experience, including serving as Superintendent of Seneca Township High School. When not leading, writing, or speaking, Dan spends his leisure time with his family, boating or chasing his kids around athletic fields, courts, and golf courses. An ardent promoter of building school cultures, developing championship programs, elevating and supporting leaders, Dan is a retired Hall of Fame softball coach and award winning Superintendent. In addition to leading his district with Irish Pride, Dan also coaches leaders in his ~~Stressed~~ Leaders Community.

How to connect with Dan:
Linked In: https://www.linkedin.com/in/dan-stecken/
Website: stressedleaders.com

More Books by Road to Awesome

Taking the Leap: A Field Guide for Aspiring School Leaders by Robert F. Breyer

Transform: Techy Notes to Make Learning Sticky by Debbie Tannenbaum

Becoming Principal: A Leadership Journey & The Story of School Community by Dr. Jeff Prickett

Elevate Your Vibe: Action Planning with Purpose by Lisa Toebben

#OwnYourEpic: Leadership Lessons in Owning Your Voice and Your Story by Dr. Jay Dostal

The Design Thinking, Entrepreneurial, Visionary Planning Leader: A Practical guide for Thriving in Ambiguity by Dr. Michael Nagler

Becoming the Change: Five Essential Elements to Being Your Best Self by Dan Wolfe

inspired: moments that matter by Melissa Wright

Foundations of Instructional Coaching: Impact People, Improve Instruction, Increase Success by Ashley Hubner

Out of the Trenches: Stories of Resilient Educators by Dana Goodier

Principled Leader by Bobby Pollicino

Road to Awesome: The Journey of a Leader
by Darrin Peppard

When Calling Parents Isn't Your Calling: A teacher's guide to communicating with all parents
by Crystal Frommert

Struggle to Strength: Finding the Ingredients to Your Secret Sauce
by Kip Shubert

Guiding Transformational Change in Education
by Kristina V. Mattis

Be the Cause: An Educator's Guide to EFFECTive Instruction
by Josh Korb

Called to Empower
by Coach Kurt Hines

The Blueprint: Survive and Thrive as a School Administrator
by Todd M. Bloomer

Sustaining Excellence: How Culture Drives Teacher Retention
by Martin Silverman

Lead with HOPE: Building a System of Self-Efficacy
by Dr. Brandi Kelly

Frogs and Crayons
by Geoffrey May

CHILDREN'S BOOKS FROM ROAD TO AWESOME

Road to Awesome A Journey for Kids
by Jillian DuBois and Darrin M. Peppard

Emersyn Blake and the Spotted Salamander
by Kim Collazo

Theodore Edward Makes a New Friend
by Alyssa Schmidt

I'm Autistic and I'm Awesome
by Derek Danziger

Emersyn Blake and the Stalked Jellyfish
by Kim Collazo

Birdie & Mipps
by Barbara Gruener

Teddy the Tiny Tree
by Derek Danziiger

roadtoawesome.net/books

www.ingramcontent.com/pod-product-compliance
Lightning Source LLC
Chambersburg PA
CBHW072158160426
43197CB00012B/2438